Jack Mitchell is the CEO of Mitchells/Richards/Marshs, three of the most successful clothing stores in the business. He and his wife, Linda, live in Wilton, Connecticut, where they raised four sons.

D1152734

www.**rbooks**.co.uk

Praise for
Hug Your People

'There ought to be more books like this on the shelves ... Divided into five parts that outline how to treat people, build trust, develop pride in your organization and be inclusive and recognize people, the book looks at how creating a niceness culture can help to create employees that stick around the company and take a personal interest in the organization ... While such changes may seem subtle, the spirit behind them is surely a very worthwhile reminder of how to make work more enjoyable for everyone'
Publishers Weekly

'*Hug Your People* is totally inspiring. Jack Mitchell takes you on a journey that is as much about life as it is about business. This book will not only help you become a better leader but also make you a better person. If you want a more rewarding relationship with another human being, read this book'
Howard Behar, author and a director of Starbucks

'If you look behind the scenes at any business that succeeds over the long term, you will find motivated, committed, energized employees. Jack Mitchell is the grand master at motivating and inspiring employees to perform brilliantly – and exceed their customers' expectations every time'
Richard J. Harrington, President and CEO, The Thomson Corporation

'Jack Mitchell explains how simple ideas, put into practice, will let your employees know how much you value them'
Ken Blanchard, coauthor, *The One Minute Manager* and *Raving Fans*

'It's about honest recognition, and basic connections with one another. Simple, yes. But difficult to find companies that actually DO it. And those that do, reap the rewards'
Career Coaching

Also by Jack Mitchell

HUG YOUR CUSTOMERS: The Proven Way to
Personalize Sales and Achieve Astounding Results

JACK MITCHELL

Hug Your People

The Proven Way to Hire,
Inspire, and Recognize
Your Team and
Achieve Remarkable Results

BANTAM BOOKS

LONDON • TORONTO • SYDNEY • AUCKLAND • JOHANNESBURG

TRANSWORLD PUBLISHERS
61–63 Uxbridge Road, London W5 5SA
A Random House Group Company
www.rbooks.co.uk

HUG YOUR PEOPLE
A BANTAM BOOK: 9780553820089

Originally published in the United States of America by Hyperion Books
First publication in Great Britain
Bantam edition published 2009

Copyright © John R. Mitchell 2008

 Hug Your Customers and Hug Your People are service
marks owned or licensed by John R. Mitchell.

John R. Mitchell has asserted his right under the Copyright, Designs and Patents Act
1988 to be identified as the author of this work.

A CIP catalogue record for this book
is available from the British Library.

This book is sold subject to the condition that it shall not,
by way of trade or otherwise, be lent, resold, hired out,
or otherwise circulated without the publisher's prior
consent in any form of binding or cover other than that
in which it is published and without a similar condition,
including this condition, being imposed on the
subsequent purchaser.

Addresses for Random House Group Ltd companies outside the UK
can be found at: www.randomhouse.co.uk
The Random House Group Ltd Reg. No. 954009

Typeset in New Baskerville

2 4 6 8 10 9 7 5 3

Penguin Random House is committed to a sustainable future for
our business, our readers and our planet. This book is made from
Forest Stewardship Council® certified paper.

Printed and bound in Great Britain by Clays Ltd, Elcograf S.p.A.

TO ALL OF OUR FABULOUS PEOPLE . . .

the 234 "huggers" . . . and their spouses and families . . .

and to all the thousands of others who made their mark working

with us since Mom and Dad opened our doors fifty years ago.

Thank you from the bottom of my heart.

MITCHELLS/RICHARDS/MARSHS
HUGGING TEAM

Aggie Auguste, Alana New, Alethea Gordon, Alina Ayrapetova, Allison Borowy, Allison Santopietro, Amy Jarman, Ana Naulaguari, Ana Margarit Tomai, Andrew Mitchell, Angela Guitard, Angela Pieretti, Angelo Pasqua, AnneMarie Drumgold, Anthony Renzuella, Arlene Pressman, Arlyne Goldberg, Barbara Evans, Belinda Cole, Beth Massoud, Be Betsy Rojas, Betty Candia, Beverly Martin, Bill Mitchell, Bob Carella, Bob Castonguay, Bob Mitchell, Bob Palazzo, Bozana Mican, Brian Hawkins, Bruce Johnson, Bruce Kelly, Bruce Lagerfeldt, Carlos Morales, Carmela Roach, Carol Mattutat, Carson Chinn, Cathy Fotinopoulos, Cathy Kozak, Chris Herde, Chris Mitchell, Christine Koster, Claire Gladstone, Claudia Henao Builes, Colleen Kenny, Courtney Duke, Dan Cote, Dan Farrington, Daniel Beliard, Danuta Dziadura, Darinka Stojanivic, David Borowy, David Hays, David Lynn, Debbie Mazza, Deborah Turtoro,

Debra Gampel, Debra O'Shea, Denise Laimo, Dennis Riordan, Derrick Lopez, Domenic Condoleo, Doreen Nugent, Dorothy Wasley, Ed Barroso, Edit Kovacs, Eleni Hasiotis, Eliza Epifano, Elizabeth Starr, Ellen Finlayson, Elli Koumbaros, Elsa Lara, Emmanuel Garcon, Enza Arella, Eric Hollo, Evelyn Shelton, Fabio Ramirez, Jr., Fatima Salvador, Ferdie Ocasio, Frank Gallagi, Gail Sheriff, Gary Barrows, Gerald Eugene, Gerry Federici, Gerry Kostic, Ginger Kermian, Giovanna Stella, Gloria Serna, Greg Alston, Hector Morales, Heidi Williams, Helene Cote, Hernando Aguila, Iren Vass, Isabel Terranova, Iwona Kelly, Jack Mitchell, Jacquie Carlino, Jacquie Tolkin, James Cash, Janet Wilson, Jay Hanna, Jean Debreus, Jean Evans, Jeff Kozak, Jennifer Celli, Jill Olson, Jim Arndt, Jim Callaghan, Jim Denino, JoAnn Salvioli, Joe Biondi, Joe Cox, Joe Derosa, Joe D'Eufemia, John Hickey III, John Hytros, Jordan Lewis, Jose Garcia, Josette Ollivierre, Judy Barker, Judy Brooks, Kim Thi, Kristen Fernandez, Kristin Hulet, Lauren Monin, Lauren Perez, Laurie Baik, Linda Arbeit-Rait, Linda Gans, Linda Levy, Linda Mitchell, Lisa Coppotelli, Lisa Iselin, Lisa Prisco, Luigi Sposito, Luis Bedoya, Lynn Tate, Maggie Yavarian, Manuel Naulaguari, Margaret Franke, Margarita Gutierrez, Margo Bonner, Maria Abrantes, Maria Sabino, Marilyn Wallack, Mark Taylor, Marlene Bernikow, Marlowe Malouf, Martha Potts, Mary Berliner, Mary Nicolia, Mary Ellen Hart, Matilde Cruz, Melissa Piorkowski, Michael Crookhorn, Michael Laszlo, Michael Servidio, Michele Romano, Nadia Kappel, Naki Halepas, Nancy Keller, Nasra Capar, Neil Gordon, Nina Prodromidis, Noella Duh, Nora Bedoya, Norberto Barroso, Pam Madonia, Pamela Miles, Pat Giannitti, Patricia Cinquemani, Patricia

Kaylor, Paul Mendelsohn, Phuong Heitz, Phyllis Bershaw, Ralph Alfano, Ray Cerritelli, Regina Cole, Richard Laidlaw, Rickee Oleet, Rita Roman, Rob Rich, Robert Greenfield, Robin Fanoli, Robin Imbrogno, Rocco Messina, Ron Marsh, Rosa Chuquimamani, Rosa Lee Jones, Rosario Ramirez, Russ Mitchell, Said Lawoo, Sam Anderson, Sandra Nacewicz, Sarah Butterfield, Scott Mitchell, Scott Nugent, Shirley Bond, Sol Lynch, Sonia Spencer, Sophia Carella, Soula Kalomenidas, Stefan Rastawiecki, Stephanie Oshana, Stephen Goss, Steve Kerman, Steve Palumbo, Sue Cammarota, Sylvia Lundberg, Sylvie Sanchez, Taffy Parisi, Teresa Baginska, Teresa Pagliuso, Theresa Cirino, Theresa Goncalves, Tia Powell, Todd Bonner, Todd Mitchell, Tom Maleri, Toni Bentley, Tony Famiglietti, Tony Gregorio, Trish Rapoport, Tullio Giannitti, Tullio Giannitti Jr., Turkan Rahim, Tyler Mitchell, Vanna Temares, Vicki Cox, Will Daley, Wilson Montaleza, Winnie Rogers, Yuriy Ayrapetov

CONTENTS

PART ONE: Nice

IT'S HOW YOU TREAT ONE ANOTHER

PART THREE: Pride

THE POWER OF ALL OF US

PART FOUR: Include

THE FIVE I'S

CONTENTS

PART FIVE: Recognize

IT'S NOT ONLY ABOUT MONEY

Welcome to the world of hugging!

Hope you enjoy reading *Hug Your People*. I would love to hear from you—feedback, comments, favorite hugging stories . . . how reading the book has influenced your business practices and the results you've achieved.
Thank you!

Hugs,

Jack

Jack Mitchell

P.S. For lots more hugs, please visit my Web site:
www.hugyourpeople.com

PROLOGUE

Everyone Wants to Be Appreciated

It's something I'd encountered before, and yet it still really jolted me—frankly, it blew me away!

Not long ago, a fabulous woman came to work for us at one of our clothing stores in Connecticut, after several years selling shirts and ties at another leading specialty store in New York City. At her last job, by anyone's definition, she was a real superstar. She worked hard, putting in endless extra hours without complaint. Her customers adored her. She made good money. The fringe benefits were generous.

So we had to wonder, why in the world did she want to leave New York City and join our team in Connecticut?

It was simple.

Nobody at the other company ever let her know in any sort of *personal* way that she was valued. Even after selling a million dollars' worth of merchandise in just one year—and that's an awful lot of shirts and ties—no one, not a single person, ever came up to her and said, "Wow, great job! You're terrific."

No! Not once! Never, ever!

Did her boss ever send her a bouquet of flowers in gratitude? Not a single daisy.

And that hurt. It made her job feel like, oh well, a job.

Her experience reminded me of something I've always understood that is very simple: **Everyone wants to be appreciated!**

I'm the CEO of a third-generation upper-end men's and women's specialty clothing business with three large stores in the New York metropolitan area. I feel blessed to have the opportunity, along with our team of wonderful people, to engage in a personal way on the selling floor with many of the hundreds and hundreds of customers who frequent our stores. I wrote a book about how my family and our associates built our business by being passionate about establishing extraordinary personal relationships that exceed expectations. It was called *Hug Your Customers.* I wrote it because it seemed to me that a lot of companies say they care about customers, but they really don't know how to show it. I thought that by sharing our stories they might learn how we show it by giving lots of hugs.

Of course a "hug" can be a bear hug, but more often it's a metaphor for what we do. We think of a hug as any positive act, gesture, or deed that personalizes a relationship and creates a "Wow, these people really care about me" feeling.

Hugging, in fact, is an extraordinarily powerful mind-set. I remember when our boys were growing up, I was dragged to see *Star Wars,* and I still can't tell Luke from Darth Vader, but I do remember someone saying, "May the Force be with you." The idea of the Force stuck with me, and I think of "hugging" as a Force.

I had no idea what the reaction to *Hug Your Customers* would be. But I've been simply astonished by its reception and by how many businesses—from Midas to Payless ShoeSource, to Nike to Morgan Stanley; from companies in Denver and Kansas City and Las Vegas, to companies in London and Stockholm and Rome and, would you believe, Estonia!—have invited me to speak to their teams because they found something meaningful and fresh in the guiding principles practiced on the floors of two Connecticut clothing stores, Mitchells and Richards. In 2005, we went ahead and acquired a third store called Marshs, on Long Island, and we've been very successfully introducing our hugging culture there as well.

But what really amazed me is that audiences were eager for more.

Again and again, I would hear the same question from people everywhere, from Starbucks to storefront delis: "How do you hire and motivate your people so they will remain productive?"

In fact, I pointed out that we "hug our people," and we actually have associates who have remained productive and loyal for thirty-five and forty-five years. They don't ever want to leave!

Numerous e-mails continue to pour in daily, and caring, ordinary, working folks march up to me after my talks, or on airplanes or in large stores, as well as at banks and real estate offices, and say, "There seems to be no loyalty anymore. Work is just not what it used to be!"

Giving great personalized customer service has always been the foremost goal of my family—we've been hugging away since my parents, Norma and Ed Mitchell, founded the business in 1958—and one thing we never lose sight of is that you can deliver great service only if you treat your associates right. You don't give extraordinary customer service in a vacuum—great people give great, personalized service!

We make a point of calling our employees "associates," because along with the fact that we value them so much, we don't like the sometimes demeaning connotations of *employee* and *worker* and, for sure, *help*. We especially like to refer to them as our "huggers," since they're the ones who embrace our customers—figuratively and literally.

Studies show convincingly—and the success of our stores are living proof—that when associates are extremely satisfied, then customers are extremely satisfied. And yet when you travel around and encounter people, whether they're selling dresses or accordions, you often see anything but satisfaction. You see people who are often surly and disgruntled, probably because they're treated shabbily, and so they treat you, the customer, shabbily—or worse, they don't acknowledge or even help you at all!

Motivating the workforce is clearly a huge global challenge. I'm simply flabbergasted by the tone of desperation that I hear from many managers and associates as they struggle to keep morale up at their companies.

I do believe with all my heart and soul that most business

leaders are honest and nice most of the time. And they work very hard and are deserving of the big bucks when they are responsible and accountable for leading their troops to achieve high profits for their stockholders, and when they also recognize and reward their associates accordingly.

And every company presumably wants successful, loyal workers. Corporate leaders say so, and of course many truly "get it" that *people* are their most important asset. Some recognize, as we do, that they are in the people business. Yet it appears to me that others focus only on hugging their product and on making a better widget, golf ball, or high-definition TV, or on painting it a different color and putting some new bells and whistles on it. Or when sales are lagging, they focus on price. They lower it and create some kind of fantastic deal—never thinking that if they treated their associates with greater personal care, they would work harder and smarter and would feel like going the extra mile to hug a customer because they feel hugged themselves!

I'm not saying you shouldn't focus on building a better product, but positive people power is fundamental to the overall success of any business.

What a tremendous difference it would make if everyone got that!

BECOMING PEOPLE-CENTRIC

These days, there's often a very serious disconnect in business. I call it a human disconnect. People spend more time at the office than at home and want to feel *personal and professional* satisfaction from their daily work experience. It's not only about the money. They want a pat on the back when they've earned it. They want the opportunity to grow to improve themselves. They want to be recognized and to feel that they have a sense of purpose at work. Not to mention that bright young people, and even a few old-timers, also want "a life."

Again, it comes down to appreciation. To our way of thinking, appreciation is everything. Even Matt Lauer on the *Today* show, after a segment on job satisfaction and recognition, signed off by saying, "A few kind words every once in a while would be nice."

From my own encounters shopping for groceries or a new car, or traveling on a plane or train, it's obvious that the need to hug your "huggers" has never been greater. All the time, I encounter people with these vacant looks that tell me that they're physically present but mentally elsewhere, because they're not engaged.

I've been amazed that in discussions with people of all ages and seniority and in every imaginable industry, very few say that they can be themselves, their *real* selves, at work. Most say they're always on guard, looking over their shoulders. Business cultures should allow people to be who they are: sincere, open, and honest, and behaving in a caring way toward one another. Companies need to recognize and build on the unique talents and strengths of each individual. It makes me very sad that so many people in the world feel they can't be genuine and can't be themselves in the workplace.

Often, the only time an employee hears from his boss is when he screws up and gets reamed out. You know, it's easy to put someone down. Some would say that the tough part is to build someone up. The reality is that it can be the most satisfying work a manager can do.

Believe me, I know. I've got a touch of dyslexia, and when I was in junior high school I was told by the guidance counselor that I would never be able to go to college because I was such a slow reader. He suggested that I ought to think about becoming a shop teacher. Thank goodness, I had great teachers who believed in me, complimented me, and helped me, and I'm proud to say I went to college and graduate school and found the right profession for me. The world certainly needs competent shop teachers, but I haven't a clue how to teach someone to make a bench or a birdcage!

The hug-your-people culture clearly enables you to be yourself. And to grow intellectually, emotionally, and financially. You are who you are, and we celebrate that.

Of course, it starts at the top. It's the leader or leaders who own the challenge and set the tone, mind-set, and culture of the company. And you, too, can be a leader of your own actions and your own destiny if you get the force of the hugging culture. I believe that leadership is not only paramount, it's *everything*.

And when hugging permeates a company, it becomes a people-centric culture.

KNOW WHAT SHELLY AND RICHARD WANT

I continue to hear from others in companies that aren't people-centric that employers barely know the individuals who carry on the work, and they surely don't know about the personal concerns so germane to their lives. They don't know that Shelly is worried because she's desperately saving to buy a house in a better school district. They don't know that Richard wishes he could have a couple of Fridays off during the summer to go spelunking or a couple of extra days in January to go snowboarding. They don't know that Carson is concerned about her teenage daughter's drinking problem. They don't know that Anthony put his mother in a nursing home last weekend. They don't even know that Elizabeth prefers to be called Lisa.

Companies don't get it that it's not nearly enough to have periodic employee recognition programs. What really matters to people is not the occasional plaque with their names embossed in gold that gets hung on their walls. It's how they are treated every day. It's the little things, the little hugs. The appreciation and attention that don't cost a dime.

For instance, you'll find out that if you smile when you say hi to someone, he or she will smile right back. Try it, it's easy to do. Smiles are not only free, they tend to multiply!

What really makes these hugs special is their context—if they're personalized they will have a more memorable meaning. If you're going to send the credit manager flowers as an expression of thanks, it's important to find out whether she likes petunias, black-eyed Susans, or lilies—don't just have the florist send a "nice bouquet." And before you place the order, make sure she isn't allergic to pollen.

That's what we strive to do at Mitchells/Richards/Marshs. We get to know our associates as if they were family, because we actually believe they are members of our extended family. When I share this, people say, "You're kidding, really?"

Time and again in conversations or even during a performance review, our associates say that they feel like they are part of the Mitchell family. It may sound corny but it's true. And personally, nothing pleases me more!

In a multitude of ways, we show our associates that we appreciate them and care about them. And we take every opportunity to enjoy one another, too. Just for fun we've had a Texas hold 'em night, we play word games, and in the spring we cheer on the Mitchells/Richards softball team! Whenever it's someone's birthday, I send the person a personalized birthday card to his or her home, and on their special day in the store we'll bring out a cake, light the candles, and eat up.

And so people arrive and stay, smiling all the way. They look forward to coming in, and they're in no hurry for their day to end. Why? They're happy. We meet their personal and financial needs, but most of all they feel engaged and important. Work, for them, is fun. That's almost a dirty word at many businesses, but it's the operative word and practice at ours.

Because people like working with us (I deliberately use *with* and not *for*) our customers enjoy shopping with us. And that ultimately gives our family business a great return on investment (ROI). We've been told by our vendors and bankers that this is undoubtedly one of our secrets of success. I mentioned in my first book that our sales were over $65 million in 2003, and we have been strongly and steadily growing ever since. But we also achieve something far more enriching than a huge increase in sales and return on investment—we enjoy a fabulous return on people (ROP)! Today we are a team of more than 250 wonderful huggers, including more than 50 seamstresses and tailors in our three stores.

THE MITCHELL BLUEPRINT

So from the feedback I've received, I'm convinced that companies and businesses need and want a detailed but simple blueprint that tells them how to assemble a happy and effective workforce that doesn't desert them the minute the business across the street offers $10 more a week or an extra vacation day.

And so this book is the Mitchell blueprint for how to hug your people.

After spending a lifetime selling suits and socks and stockings alongside Mom and Dad (God rest their souls); my brother, Bill; my wife, Linda; and our four sons and three nephews, I've recognized that there are five broad principles that guide us in hugging our people. And when I say "people," I mean everyone who works with us—the sales and customer service associates on the selling floors, the cleaning staff, the delivery people, our buyers and tailors, the backroom financial wizards, the marketing and advertising people, our advisory board, and also the outsourced people like our human resources specialists. I'm even talking about our mailmen, FedEx and UPS guys, and our friends at IBM and Pitney Bowes.

I'm a big believer in the power of positive words and actions, and so the names of these principles are carefully chosen to reflect a larger message. They are

NICE

TRUST

PRIDE

INCLUDE

RECOGNIZE

Now, they may not sound like the principles you've heard before from self-help business books, but they're the ones that have worked mightily for us and they'll work for you! They're intrinsically linked and form a powerful and synergistic force. They are sound and solid, and they produce astounding results. The energy and enthusiasm behind, and execution of, these principles are tremendous and enduring at Mitchells/ Richards/Marshs.

Each principle is something that I feel is essential to convey to all of the people who work with us. My guiding principles are to be Nice to them, to Trust them, to instill Pride in them, to Include them, and to generously Recognize them.

If you succeed in all five of these principles, then you will produce loyal and effective associates and the strongest of strong teams. They key is personalization delivered positively with passion. Once you have that magical connection on a personal level, the rest is just focusing with great discipline on consistency and execution and delivery.

I'm not saying we're perfect—no one is—and we have had our blips, but people have told us, "Jack, you and your family have created a very special culture here."

In the following pages, I will take you through these five principles to convey what we mean by each of them and to share some true stories that show how they are implemented. I'll fill you in on novel concepts we've developed, such as the Five I's and reconnect and checking in, and a nifty little exercise I'm partial to called Going to the Moon!

None of these concepts are abstract ideas worked out on a blackboard or on a computer screen. I believe we live these principles. We live them every day in real time. I know they work, because I've seen them work—for decades and with hundreds of talented people who have graced our floors and say they love coming to work!

These principles are applicable to any industry and to any size company, be it small, medium, large, or even 2XL. And I believe they're globally transferable. They'll work on the factory floor of a baked-bean plant or at a hairpin wholesaler. They'll work in an insurance or real estate agency or stock brokerage. They'll work in a small family business as well as at a multinational giant.

The world may conduct business in 6,800 languages, but everyone understands and loves a hug.

As was true in *Hug Your Customers*, *Hug Your People* contains real stories about real people—a commonsense book, based on examples of associates being nice to one another, trusting one another, feeling pride in their environment and the people they work with, being included, and getting recognized.

At the end of each section, I've included a Hugging Study Guide that sums up the important points mentioned. And at the conclusion of the book I've brought back the Hugging Achievement Test (HAT), a fun exercise to help you absorb the information.

When I think about how our company operates, I return to a comment that Nick Donofrio, executive vice president for innovation and technology at IBM, made to me: "At the end of the day I ask myself, did I make a difference today?"

It reminds me of something that Dad said to himself with the same sentiment and in almost the same words when he woke up each day: "I hope I can make a difference to our people today."

I sincerely hope that this book will make a difference for you, too, so that you and your company will be inspired to truly hug your people. I dream that you'll hug the chap or kid or old man in the next office or cubicle or at the office meeting. You'll smile and say thanks by bringing in some cupcakes or a jar of pickles. You'll go for it and make a difference with an unexpected or surprise hug that will light up the room and another person's spirit.

It's worked for us—across three generations and fifty years—and it'll work for you.

And work will never, ever seem like work again.

PART ONE

Nice

It's How You Treat One Another

CHAPTER 1

Building a Niceness Culture

Years ago I learned about the three levels of knowledge, or the Three K's, a nifty way of framing your awareness of a subject. Whenever I'm tussling with an important issue, the Three K's spring to mind.

The three levels of knowledge go like this:

- **K1:** You know what you know.
- **K2:** You know what you don't know.
- **K3:** You don't know what you don't know—the scariest of them all!

Here's an easy way to understand the paradigm:

You know what you know: I know that penicillin is a miracle antibiotic used to treat common diseases and ward off infections.

You know what you don't know: I know I don't know anything about the chemical structure of penicillin or the actual process by which it slays disease or (until I just looked it up) that the best strain of it came from a moldy cantaloupe found in a garbage can.

You don't know what you don't know: There are dozens of so-called uncontacted tribes in the world isolated from the rest of civilization that don't even know that penicillin exists and could prevent them from dying from wounds and ailments—so they don't know what they don't know.

The Three K's hit me like a ton of bricks whenever I contemplate corporate cultures. It's so often the case, especially in companies that fail to achieve their potential, that you don't know what you don't know. And what's troubling is that this happens with the most critical building block of a business.

Lots of companies seem stuck in the third level of knowledge when it comes to the importance of being nice to their associates. They don't know that associates are the foundation of success. Instead, they regard them as an expense item, especially if they have a pension fund, like the airlines. A senior flight attendant said to me recently, "I used to feel like an asset, and now I definitely feel like a liability."

That's a huge contrast to an organization like Starbucks, which from the very beginning offered part-time associates health benefits! I once heard a barista say, "They give me flexible hours plus health insurance!"

And then there are companies that are trapped in the second level of knowledge. They know the value of their associates but don't know how to show them they are appreciated. At our company, we know that the most important asset we have is our people, and we aim to demonstrate this on a daily basis through what I think of as a Niceness Culture.

Just the other day, I was at the bottom of what I call the Stairway to Heaven at our Richards store, which leads to the women's selling floor, and I turned to Rob Rich, a sales associates who has been with us for many, many years and who was having a breakout year, and I simply shook his hand and said, "Great job, Rob! You're really doing outstanding. Thanks so much!" It was a spontaneous act on my part, one that now seems to come naturally to me, because he *is* doing a great job, and I know this little acknowledgment made him feel like a million bucks. And his sales are continuing to increase.

We do things like this all the time. I've watched Debra Gampel do it, and so many others, because they've learned the power of simple, straightforward praise. We all try to be nice.

Now, I don't know of any company that thinks of itself as being deliberately cruel to its associates, or even chilly to them, but how many companies actually have as part of their corporate strategy the intention to be nice and to routinely acknowledge how valuable their associates are? Not many. As a result, few truly produce a Niceness Culture. Starting at the top, you have to encourage niceness through deliberate and proactive gestures and activities until you produce an environment where people are genuinely and consistently considerate toward one another.

A lot of people get the idea of a Niceness Culture from their mothers or fathers, or maybe from a nursery school teacher or a beloved babysitter, and they recognize its absence in many corporate climates and yearn for it. Over the years, several people have told us our environment is so nice that their colleagues often make them feel even better than they feel at home. That means you might come from a somewhat dysfunctional family and recognize that the store is a place that feels like the functional home environment you've always wished for. And if you are from a functional home, you recognize it as an extension of home.

Of course, if you're used to being beaten up for making mistakes or being ordered around all the time, it can take time to adjust. You're always thinking you're going to get fired or the other shoe is going to drop if you admit you're having a hard time making your targets, because every time you didn't do it right at home in your sadly dysfunctional family you got smacked or put down.

But once you get accustomed to a Niceness Culture, you feel uplifted—"put up" not "put down"—and believe me, you'll never want to leave it, ever.

What, then, is a Niceness Culture? It's a culture where these three things are true:

1. There's a "pleaser" mentality.
2. Relationships are personalized.
3. There is humility.

There's a "pleaser" mentality—by this, we mean that people want to do nice things just to be nice. The mind-set is that everyone in the organization has consistently great manners that are used to please others. When they interact, managers and associates use expressions such as "excuse me," "please," and "Can I help you?"—positive phrases that suggest that we all strive to please one another.

With a pleaser mentality, people are always looking to give coworkers a helping hand. Fabio will say to Stephen, "Go home early, I know it's your son's birthday, I'll gladly cover for you," and the next month Stephen will turn to Fabio and say, "I know you want to play in that softball game, I'll take that urgent order down to UPS so it gets out to California tonight. Go ahead." More often than not, a pleasing act comes back to hug you just when you need it.

It's very important that people are *consistently* polite to one another, not only when it's a nice day out. Even when it's raining or a blizzard is coming down, people who are polite remain polite. Mom used to take politeness to a new level. She would write thank-you notes in response to thank-you notes. We used to kid her, "Mom, they're thanking *you*. Why are you thanking *them?*" And she would say, "I like to."

What's also true is that, hopefully, no one ever does something hurtful to another person in a premeditated and manipulative manner. For instance, a nice person would never, ever use the word *hate*. One day I was describing how I hated to eat fish when Lyle, my oldest grandson, turned to me and said, "Grandpa, *hate* is a swear word." I couldn't agree more; it's not a polite thing to say. I really *dislike* fish, though. I far prefer chicken—in fact, I love chicken.

Possibly the greatest pleaser I ever knew was my grand-mother on my mother's side. She always gave so much—whether it was lessons in canasta or a much-needed loan—without ever expecting anything back, other than she loved to hear how we shared her boundless gifts with others. She gave us the "gift of giving," which Bill and I, with our spouses, have tried to pass on from generation to generation. And now we play gin rummy, poker, or bridge with our families. My grandmother lived to be eighty-nine, and always wore a big smile on her face, even in her later years when she was in a wheelchair. Bill affectionately called her Sunflower.

Relationships are personalized—this means that people en-gage one another as real people rather than as job responsibil-ities. They get to know Ralph not as a shoe buyer but as someone who likes to go kayaking and has eight-year-old twin girls. Michael's not accounts receivables, but a marathoner who loves mango pudding. We think of these as *whole* relationships rather than *partial* relationships. In a whole relationship, peo-ple forge a personal bond. That's critical, because we believe that if you don't have personalization in the professional rela-tionship there can be no effective communication. And with-out communication, you've got a dead organization.

If you're the head of marketing and I'm the head of sales and we come together only to share great ideas, can we move the company forward? Or do we need to personalize the rela-tionship in some manner? I can't conceive of working with someone with whom I didn't take some time to see and know as a whole person.

To a large extent, it comes down to empathy. Early in my business career, I thought you just had to *understand* someone— but I later learned that empathy is a broader and more meaningful concept than understanding. Feeling empathy results in what I call the Five C's:

Caring

Compassion

Cooperativeness

Consistency

Cash (Just kidding! Simply checking to see if you're still with me on empathy)

Personalizing relationships means you try to figure out what's important to everyone and how they feel, and to find a unique way to "hug" them that makes them think, *Wow, they care about me, they truly care about me, this is such a nice place to work.*

You can alter a blue blazer or sell aluminum siding at many places, but in order to be nice to the person in the cubicle next to yours, you need to personalize the relationship by knowing about their aspirations and tribulations, and then to demonstrate that you genuinely care about them.

How well do you know your colleagues, your coworkers? And how many do you *really* know?

There is humility—this is a tremendously unappreciated value. Everyone's heard of companies where the big shots fly business and first class while the underlings fly coach on the same plane. Or where some of the leaders and managers are prima donnas and self-centered, and yet are constantly demanding this or that from their workers without taking time to recognize how hard their employees work. Under that sort of harsh leadership, work becomes just a job, not a career, and there's little or no loyalty at all to coworkers or to the company.

Our definition of *humility* is an environment where people, especially leaders and managers, don't think they know it all and everyone is not only willing but encourages others to succeed. It's never saying about yourself or your business that you're "the best," but behaving as if there is room for new ideas. The leaders have no problem saying, "I don't know" or "Now that you've pointed that out, I've changed my mind." It means standing behind someone, not stealing credit for ideas that weren't yours, and enabling others to shine rather than always grabbing the spotlight. There's a sense of togetherness and of putting others' needs ahead of your own. It means fessing up to mistakes. It means apologizing.

Now, these things aren't necessarily easy to do, and we're not always perfect at them—in fact, many times it's downright difficult to remember to do them unless they come naturally to you. But they really matter.

When there's humility, everyone is also encouraged to feel as equal as possible. That means thinking of others first, or certainly as equal, regardless of whether you have superiority in rank or position. We're not big on titles. My brother, Bill, likes to use "Coach" on his business cards, and introduces himself as "your favorite socks salesman." Using first names is a simple form of humility for us. On occasion, people will call me Mr. Mitchell, and I ask them to please call me Jack. To have to call the boss "Mr." seems uncomfortable and demeaning. From our standpoint, it's very important to do everything possible to level the playing field between the boss and others.

WE'RE ALL FRIENDS

Ultimately, when all three of these ingredients—pleaser mentality, personalized relationships, humility—are present, people often become friends with their coworkers, friends who truly like and root for one another. And that's why when Debbie Mazza noticed how frenetically busy Angie was at work, staying late and sometimes missing meals at home, Debbie called Angie one evening and said, "Listen, I'm coming over with a meatloaf, so your husband will have something for dinner." Angie was incredibly touched that Debbie had thought of her and her husband's stomachs—and the meatloaf was absolutely delicious!

Not a day—or even an hour—goes by that I don't regard our associates as my friends. And in a true Niceness Culture, this sentiment flows in all directions. Top down (leaders to troops), sideways (peers to peers), and bottom up (troops to leaders). The Niceness Culture must span the entire "bandwidth" of the company.

And it's the function of leadership to manage this. For instance, if someone is crossing the line and being a dash too nasty or, God forbid, "ugly" (and I realize the vast majority of time people don't know they are being nasty), it's time to quietly and privately talk to them about it.

When you achieve a Niceness Culture, it will attract great, positive people who won't ever leave. And it will improve productivity, because people work their best when they feel great. When people are appreciative of the joyful environment, they reciprocate. And then they hug your customers, the vendors, the mailman, and on and on. We have this great mailman at Richards named Glen, as well as a great UPS driver named Kurt, and a great FedEx driver named Gary. They feel like part of our team, too, because we're nice to them. It's amazing how they hug us back when we have an emergency. Somehow they always find that lost package or letter we so dearly need.

It's always a wonderful, positive comment about our stores when a customer remarks, "You have the nicest people working with you, and everyone seems to get along with everyone so well." And we agree with them and say, "There's a lot of hugging going on here! Thanks for noticing!"

That's why Ed and Norma Mitchell, my parents, who started it all, said of our first tiny store, "It's a pleasant place to shop." And why I also say, "It's a pleasant place to work!"

And later, as we grew, we amended the logo line to "Once a customer, always a friend." And I like to say, "Once an associate, always a friend!"

How do we find these friends? Coming up next.

CHAPTER 2

How to Hire Nice People

Not long ago, I was giving a *Hug Your Customers* speech in Denver to Sage Hospitality Resources, one of the country's leading hotel management companies. After I finished enumerating the four qualities we look for when hiring associates, Walter Isenberg, Sage's chief executive, turned to me and said, "Jack, I have a fifth. We like to hire *nice* people."

"How do you determine nice?" I asked.

Elaborating, he said, "When you flew from New York to Denver yesterday, by the time you were cruising over St. Louis I'll bet you pretty much knew if the person sitting next to you was nice or not. You knew by noticing if she asked if she could hold your briefcase while you fit your luggage into the overhead rack, and if she never hogged the armrest, and if she politely asked you to move when she needed to powder her nose rather than just barging through, dumping your Diet Pepsi on your lap—right?"

"Of course," I replied.

Hearing this tickled me, because I realize that we also take the time and work hard to hire nice people. Because if you want to build a Niceness Culture, it helps a lot—indeed, it's essential—to start with nice associates. Believe me, it's a lot more fun working with nice people. It's also easier to be nice to nice people.

That's why we always make a point of hiring for *culture* first, not for *skills* or passion for *product*.

We would absolutely never hire anyone who had fabulous skills who we didn't think fit our culture. If someone is a great person, he can usually acquire great skills through education. But in our experience, it's very rare that someone with great skills can transform himself from a nasty to a nice person.

Of course, it's wonderful if he or she has the right skills, too—for sellers that means someone who "listens" and "mirrors" the client and makes specific proposals, and, in our case, loves clothes and is fanatical about fashion. But some of our sellers don't have a passion for fashion. However, they would die for their clients, their kids, and the hugs of appreciation customers return to them every time they are in our stores!

Now sometimes, because of your economic constraints or the availability of talent in your market, you have to hire "good" rather than "great" people. After all, you have to pay more for great people, especially if they also have great skills. During tough times, then, you should consider people with a good cultural fit and with good skills who are willing to grow to become great.

So how do you identify who to hire?

We use five criteria (I mentioned the first four in *Hug Your Customers* and have added a new one):

1. Integrity: This is the heart of our family business, and we try to detect it during the probing we do during the interview process and by giving prospective associates an "integrity test" created by Reid Psychological Systems. Integrity is deeper than whether someone will steal clothes or money, or expense something personal—and the Reid test is designed to reveal these inclinations. It's will you have the courage and confidence to speak up and candidly share your comments and criticisms (as well as praise and acknowledgments)? We like to ask: In your previous jobs, did you always trust your colleagues and your boss? How about an example or two? Were you always candid with them on all challenges that you faced? Can you tell me a story of how you handled a challenge?

2. Positive attitude: You pick up on this by whether they see the world as the glass being half empty or half full, and we like it better if they see it five-eighths or even seven-eighths full. Is the candidate constantly blaming his ex-boss or company for why he failed in a particular position, or is he smiling and recounting how he got here because of what he learned from Angela or Jean?

3. Passion to listen, learn, and grow, to be the best you can be, every day! This shows in people wanting to have a career with us, not just a job. And passionate people are those who have that proverbial "fire in the belly." We often ask, What do you like to read and what are your three to five favorite books? And your one or two favorite business books? Obviously this tells you about their commitment to learning. If they say they don't like to read, we might say, "Really?" And then move to their favorite TV or movie list, or try to determine how they absorb information to better their lives.

4. Competent and confident: You can check competence by their résumés and references, but self-confidence is equally vital, and one way you can tell if they've got it is if they have excelled at past experiences, whether it's selling Acuras or doing crossword puzzles. And what were their strengths or skill sets that enabled them to excel? Are their nonverbal actions in sync with their words and past achievements? Do they look you in the eye? Are they nervous? Of course, everyone is somewhat nervous during an interview, and we understand this, but a self-confident person will become comfortable once she begins talking about herself.

5. Nice: An absolutely essential trait that underlies all of these and that we think of as a fifth ingredient is that the people are *very, very nice*. Now, no one is going to tell you that they're mean—that they used to torment their sister and love to kick the dog—so how do you tell?

Well, you talk to them and listen to them and watch them. When they enter the room, do they embrace you with a smile, a firm handshake, and a warm demeanor? Do they open with a "How are you?" and does it sound like they really mean it and care about you? And before the conversation is over have they told a story about how they are compassionate—be it toward a friend, family member, or business associate? If they haven't, I simply say, "Blow your own horn. I like people who are proud of some of the nice things they've done. Got any stories that illustrate that you've been compassionate toward others?"

When asked this during his interview, Brian Hawkins immediately said to me, "Well, I used to take my friends at Saks and Brooks Brothers to get real soul food in New York." And I replied, "I don't know what real soul food is like, Brian." And I could just see him light up with the idea that we would eat greasy pork that was good for the soul, even if, as he kidded, it could be *murder* on the body.

Nice is simply something that you recognize when you see it. I'm sure you can think of your own, but here are some essential traits of nice that everybody ought to consider:

- Nice people are thoughtful
- Nice people are friendly
- Nice people smile
- Nice people offer to help
- Nice people are genuine
- Nice people take responsibility (they don't blame others)

You know nice when you see it, you know it when you feel it. If you don't see it or feel it, it's a good reason to pass.

ASK THESE QUESTIONS

To hire people who embody our five criteria—integrity; positive attitude; passion to listen, learn, and grow to be the best you can be every day; competent and confident; and nice—you have to be alert and curious and focused during the interview process. Keep a notepad and write down your inner thoughts. Have they offered any examples of the thrill of achievement as an individual or as a team player? Are they the co-captain of the team? Are they good listeners? Do they have a sense of humor? Are they polite?

And I really love it when the person is as curious about me and my business as I am about him. It demonstrates that he has invested the time to do research on me and our family and business and for his potential career.

Curiosity, we find, is a very valuable virtue in successful people.

We feel you ought to ask three key questions relating to each of the five principles that are the heart and soul of this book—Nice, Trust, Pride, Include, and Recognize—to tease out whether people are a fit. And when you ask them, watch and listen to both verbal and nonverbal cues. These are the questions, and be sure to make them open-ended, so they can give you a full and genuine response and hopefully tell a story or two.

NICE

1. Share with me the nicest thing you've ever done for someone.

2. How did this action feel to you?

3. Who is the nicest person you know and why? (And, of course, watch and listen for random or proactive acts of niceness.)

TRUST

1. What does trust mean to you?

2. Can you give me an example of when someone trusted you?

3. Can you think of a time when you trusted someone and it really paid off or perhaps one that didn't? (Another one, which we use only occasionally, I learned from my friend Morris Kulmer at A&K Railroad Materials: look right into their brown or blue eyes and say, "Do you always tell the truth?" I think it's a neat question to ask, although I don't want to insult the person. It's rarely answered with just a yes or no, and it's always interesting when I hear more about why they answer the way they do.)

PRIDE

1. What do you do for fun? (Here you are probing whether or not the person is proud of these outside activities and does well at them. Usually we do well in the things we have fun doing. Then you can ask follow-up questions to determine if they are leaders, team players, investors, active participants, or spectators. If they can't quickly answer with several passionate activities, then we don't want this dull person on our team.)

2. What are you most proud of, whether it's something large or small? (We like to see if they are most proud of a team effort and their contribution to the "win," or only of an individual effort. There is no right or wrong answer, but since we value humility, we like it a lot when the person adds that they couldn't have done it without the support of Mom and Dad or a colleague or, in my case, Bill.)

3 Can you give me an example or a story of something you're not proud of? (I don't often ask this unless we've gotten into a dialogue during which I've shared how I made a mistake and it's something I wasn't proud of.)

INCLUDE

1. How do you make decisions? (You want to probe to see if they solicit other people's opinions.)

2. Do you value—really value—other people's opinions? Can you give me an example of how you value input from others?

3. Do you think of yourself as independent, dependent, or interdependent (the best of all)? In other words, do you walk on the beach or work out alone, or do you do it with someone else? Or do both?

RECOGNIZE

1. In what ways were you recognized at your last jobs—or not recognized? Did they recognize your strengths? Did they encourage you to grow your natural talents?

2. What are your expectations about money? (Usually, I then follow up by saying, "What was your W-2 last year?" I've even had candidates bring in W-2 forms, for two reasons: it indicates that they're honest and it enables us to be sure we compensate them fairly.) We love it when they quickly say that money isn't their only priority, which is what I believe.

3. What is it that really makes you feel appreciated at work? Any examples of how you have made others feel appreciated?

Once you've exhausted these questions, ask the person about his or her vision of the position being interviewed for. And then say, "What can you add immediately to make your mark? How about five years from now?"

We always try to have the person's potential direct manager pose the same questions, phrased a little differently, and then we check to see if the answers are similar to the previous comments. We're probing for consistency, another important quality. I also try to walk around with the person to check on his speed and quickness and how he relates to new people he meets on the floor and in other offices, which is essential to our retail business.

MULTIPLE INTERVIEWS ARE A MUST

Ever been blown away by a great first impression of someone and then later completely changed your mind? Or maybe you still like the person, but she's not quite the wow you thought she was?

That's why we do many interviews, sometimes as many as six, and it works well for both us and the prospect. We get to know them as thoroughly as we can in a short period of time, and they get to know us. One way that a bright candidate realizes that you really care about her is that you expose her to many members of your team. After all, your decision to hire her or not is a very big deal for her, perhaps even bigger than for the company. The key is that it be a great fit for both parties.

During this process, I still love to be included in at least one of the interviews, because the presence of the CEO says that the candidate is important and we care about him.

If the person has come to see me, I try to meet him at the front door rather than have my assistant bring him to my office. I always try to introduce the person to everyone we run into by her first and hopefully last name. Naturally, I offer a comfortable and quiet setting, with seating that doesn't give you a backache. The office should be reasonably neat—though I'm terrible in that department, and sometimes tell the person she might as well see it as it is, which at least shows the candidate reality. And, of course, I offer tea, coffee, Pepsi, or whatever is his pleasure (and I hope it isn't whiskey). Afterward, I walk the person back to the front door and, unless I'm really pressed for time, I walk him all the way to his car or pass him on to another colleague for the next interview.

If we are pretty sure we are going to hire the person, we ask many more questions than the ones I've already mentioned. We've been truly surprised at how much people reveal and share about themselves during this process, and it forms the foundation for a strong lifelong relationship early in the game. Once they begin to trust that we are truly interested in them, people open up. Let's face it: most people like to talk about themselves.

We often get asked, Where do you find all these nice people? Well, a lot of them apply to us. But many of our best leads emanate from our associates. Jim Arndt brought us Judy Brooks. Judy in turn brought us Jim Callahan. In our Long Island store, Lisa Prisco brought in Mary Berliner. Then Lisa and Mary brought in Arlene Pressman and Chris Koster. Then the power of all of these ladies helped bring us Angelo Pasqua and Luigi Sposito.

As you can see, the personalization of relationships is pivotal. Networking your own customer database also often leads to wonderful new associates. A year or so ago, a customer said to me, "Jack, my wife shops with Shirley Bond and she's terrific." A little while later, Shirley came into the store and we hired her soon thereafter. And for sure she is a wow!

Finally, we're always on the lookout for staff, especially great sellers, when stores go out of business. Recently Grossman's, Greenwich's leading shoe store, suddenly closed—giving its associates all of one week's notice—and we quickly hired several of its great sellers, including Sylvie and Jacquie.

Our vendor friends also function like scouts from the farm system. They're constantly alerting us to great players from

other teams with amazing batting averages and who are Gold
Glove fielders. It's their own way of being nice to us because
we've been nice to them.

So now that you've heard my suggestions for hiring great
and nice people, let's welcome them into your home!

CHAPTER 3

Forget Probation,
Get Married for Life!

We always drill into our people the importance of first impressions with customers, because everyone gets only one first impression. Well, what about first impressions with new associates? How many businesses really take those seriously?

Think about it. When a company hires a new person—whether it's a salesperson or a middle manager or a cook for the company cafeteria—it obviously has high expectations. And the new hire surely has high hopes, too. And even though supervisors normally are encouraging to new people, and new people are usually diligent and do everything possible to present the best possible face, there's a lot of wariness bubbling on both sides.

Businesses make this jitteriness all the worse by clinging to the concept of probation. At many companies, a new person is automatically placed on probation, a short-term trial period usually lasting six months to a year, before they become a full-fledged associate. The idea is that the new hire has to demonstrate that he or she has got the right stuff and is not, heaven forbid, a mistake. I don't know about you, but to us, probation suggests a convicted felon. Do you want to think of your supervisor as your probation officer?

One of our associates even told us that at a former employer the mantra was "Hire to fire." When she became a manager, she was told that after three to six months they should fire most people so that they didn't have to pay the benefits conferred to permanent employees.

Well, we never put anyone on probation or have any sort of interim orientation period. When we hire someone, the person is hired. That's why when someone joins us we think of him or her as getting *married* to us for life!

Marriage has a positive glow to it. Two people have decided they want to commit to each other and make a life together. In a job, the two parties have also made a commitment to one another. Marriages, of course, do collapse. Some couples find they really weren't meant for each other—he likes butter, she likes marmalade, and they can't work it out—and the same holds true at a company. Misjudgments are made—by either party.

But the majority of marriages endure, and they sure do in our case. And that's why when we hire someone we want them to immediately feel happy and full of high expectations, not that they're being tested to see if they pass muster.

To set the tone of the marriage, as soon as someone agrees

to our job offer we frequently send flowers to the person's home, accompanied by a personal card from the manager who hired the individual. It's totally unexpected, and it makes the new hire feel wanted.

To keep the early stages of the marriage upbeat, I sometimes celebrate short-term milestones. After Mom passed, Dad remarried late in life—at ninety, in fact—so late that he knew the odds were slim that he would be able to mark things like ten-year anniversaries, and even one-year celebrations were going to be iffy. So he and his wife, Muriel, would celebrate one-month anniversaries.

I sometimes like to do that with new associates, sending them congratulatory notes or other hugs after a month, two months, three months, to make them feel welcome. They love it. Every once in a while, I wake up in the morning and have the urge to shoot someone an e-mail and say something like I did for a new associate at Mitchells: "Wow, Carmela, you are a fabulous new addition to our women's team in Westport! Linda mentioned to me the other night, and I couldn't agree more, that in addition to being nice, you are selling across all of the collections that we have, obviously taking the time and carefully selecting each item for your/our customers. Hugs, Jack."

Right after you've hired someone, it's also imperative that you go out of your way to make the new arrival feel welcome. When a reporter is hired at *The New York Times*, a so-called desk buddy is assigned to him. He's a staffer chosen because he seems simpatico with the new person. He's asked to take the individual out to lunch (at the company's expense, naturally), and to be generally available to answer any questions. If the new reporter is from out of town, the desk buddy can fill him in on the difference between the W train and the 4 train, who has the best pizza nearby, and who's that tall guy with the pug nose on the National Desk.

It's a terrific idea, because it immediately makes someone feel like an intrinsic part of the team and relieves the anxiety of being the new guy or gal in town.

One of the best devices that we sometimes employ to get the marriage off on the right foot is a sort of early-bird bonus.

Many new workers arrive not strictly because they think they'll be happy at your company, but because they were miserable someplace else. All the time, new associates confide that they had worked their tail off and just never felt valued, and so they don't have a warm workplace feeling. You want to flush that from their systems right away.

And so a little thing we occasionally do for those who are executing their jobs in an exceptional way, or when it just feels like the right thing to do, is to give them a bonus sometime in the first six months. It's not usually anything stupendous—it might be just $100 or $300—but the impact far exceeds the actual sum. No one expects to get a bonus so soon. The universal protocol is after a year, at the earliest. And so it always comes as a very pleasant surprise. That's why I like to call it the Surprise Discretionary Hug Bonus.

We've found that it's really well received. It quickly lets the air out of the new associate's anxiety level and makes the person feel at home.

Just picture it. You call the associate in, and the person is probably pretty jittery. Did I mess up already? Boom, out of the blue you hand over a check *and* a kind word of recognition, as well as the most "touching" hug you feel is appropriate, whether a firm handshake, a high five, an actual hug—or even all three.

Without exception, the person is blown away. The little ceremony also offers an interim opportunity to have the associate open up a little about how he perceives he is doing, since he knows you wouldn't invest even $200 in him if you felt there was any reason that you were going to break the marriage vows. And a nice little side benefit is that this reassurance often causes the associate's performance to improve a notch, because he's been made to feel good.

And you know what? It also feels great signing the check, handing it over with a smile, and seeing that wonderful glow on the new associate's face. Same thing happens when you surprise them with a personalized note (and try signing it with a real ink pen)!

CHAPTER 4

Is It Kathy or Cathy?
(Cathie or Kathi?)

A good friend of mine told me this anecdote about his company that spoke volumes about its culture. One day, the chief executive was wandering around the floor of my friend's department. He was hunting for one of the supervisors, and he found her conferring with an associate. She greeted him warmly, and he reciprocated, and then he glanced at the associate with a blank look and asked the supervisor, "New hire?"

The person had been there for seven years. Can you imagine how small he felt?

He had actually been interviewed by the company head when he was hired, had greatly admired him, and had worked diligently in the hope of being recognized and moved up the corporate ladder. Now he felt crushed and demoralized. He left the company within the year.

Of course, it would have been a totally different outcome if the company head had said, "Hey, Paul, great to see you. How have you been? Any new snow globes in your collection?"

But that's not what happened, and that's not what happens at a lot of workplaces. Naturally, it's impossible for the leadership to know the name and something about everyone who works with their company, unless we're talking about a fairly small business. But top executives need to do a lot better in this area if they want to nurture a dedicated work team. We certainly feel that everyone in a managerial position needs to know his or her top 100 to 150 associates, and frankly 250 is not unreasonable. I would prioritize them in this way:

1. The person you report to
2. Those who report to you
3. Those associates who make a difference in enabling you to deliver whatever you need to do to achieve your goals

As for the people who directly report to a manager, they should know these top 100 to 150 people, too, because direct reports reflect on the manager.

And if you know even more, all the better. Bill Conaty, General Electric's senior vice president for corporate human resources, may be the champion name-knower. GE employs 625 senior executives worldwide, and Bill shared with me that he essentially knows them all—every last one. GE has 185 company officers, and Bill knows them personally, including their wives, kids, and interests. Wow!

One reason this familiarity is so important is that in larger organizations, top-level leaders are not in a position to regularly hug their "internal" customers. Certainly, someone like Jeff Immelt, the CEO at GE, can't possibly hug every associate, but he does make a huge effort. Bill helps Jeff by bringing in groups of GE executives from around the world to have round-table discussions and dialogues with Jeff. I've heard Jeff say on several occasions that he spends an enormous amount of time at the John F. Welch Leadership Development Center in Crotonville, New York, listening and learning from the new and veteran GE employees. And I know from the hundreds of GE executives that are customers of ours that because Jeff and Bill do it, they do it. They hug their people, who then hug the customers.

And, of course, Jeff and Bill know all of their top-level associates intimately—vice chairman, senior VP, assistants, the board of directors, head accountant, head attorney, and so on—and they in turn hug down the line to their internal customers.

With everyone on your to-know list, you should remember their first and last names for sure, but let's be frank: sometimes you're not introduced to someone by the person's last name, and so you need a system to find it out. In our case, we have a sign-in process on the computer that sorts by the person's first name and includes their last names, and all of our associates are also listed under our customer database. At CCA Global Partners, its employee directory even has photographs so you can link the name with the face of the person. I love that!

Now, many people say that it's just too hard to learn that many names unless you have a photographic memory. It's actually easy, if you put your mind to it. And it's like hitting a topspin or playing the piano well or learning how to scuba dive. It's all about practice. Practice, practice, and practice.

Once you know their names, don't stop there. You also need to learn a few things about them to personalize the relationship. You should gather data about them just as you glean information about your customers, even more so! We collect data on customers in three categories: business, family, and personal. We do it the same way with associates—not as formally, but we do it.

Obviously you don't gather every little tidbit down to their favorite vegetable and third-grade teacher, but you should know their spouses, the names and ages of their children, their pets, their best-liked vacation spots, their hobbies, and whether they prefer coffee, tea, or Diet Mountain Dew.

We also find it useful to ask associates what they like to do as a team—whether it's the debating team or the volleyball team. The interview process is the ideal time to do this, but of course there are other times you can gather this information as well. I also like to have them identify their professional and personal goals, as well as learning and enjoyment goals, up to three. Maybe someone wants to read more fiction or take Swahili lessons or build ships inside bottles. Why ask this? Once again, the personalization of the relationship is everything. It's amazing how revealing and interesting people's backgrounds truly are. You store this information in your head and you use it when appropriate. You know that Michael Servideo wants to read more books on cartography, so one day you send him a new book on cartography.

Patricia, a newly arrived associate, told me that her daughter was the center of the universe for her. She went mountain climbing with her, among numerous other activities. So I try to always ask her about her daughter and whether they've been tackling the mountains lately. She told me that in her previous position no one ever paid attention to that relationship before, and by my paying attention to it she feels I know her. Personalizing the relationship has a way of doing that!

Now, it's important that much of this private and privileged information is kept that way, as is the data about our customers. That's what being nice and building personal relationships requires.

And finally, nothing is as important as spelling a person's name correctly. My face was very red years ago when I sent a note to a very special person, my future first daughter-in-law, Kathryn Pamela Bowler Mitchell: "Cathy, really great to see you again!" This misspelling was simply *not* nice. I will never, ever forget that this charming Kathy is spelled with a *K*. And I've learned for sure how important it is to check and double-check the spelling of people's names!

CHAPTER 5

Making the Human Connection

Whenever I'm squirming in the dentist chair, not a place I spend any more time than my teeth insist on, Jeffrey, my hugging dentist, always turns to his technician and says, "Thanks for coming in early for Jack." He does this, of course, right in front of me, which makes it even more meaningful for his colleague. It's a straightforward enough hug. And as I gaze into the technician's eyes, I see him or her smile.

A little thing, but it's a nice thing. Over time, these little things add up. And, like most hugs, they're free.

We think of these pleasantries as forms of "connection"— human connection. When you're nice to your associates in ways that are important to them, you're connecting with them. And that's a vital part of establishing a Niceness Culture.

Of course, it's absolutely essential that these acts are genuine. Knee-jerk or calculated expressions of gratitude don't really have the same impact. By your body language and your level of enthusiasm, people can readily detect when you are just smiles and words and not deeds, and then the connections quickly disconnect.

It never hurts, though, to have a little reminder to spur you on. My son Todd was at a meeting of jewelers and met Richard Kessler, a hugging jeweler in Wisconsin. Richard told him about a nifty trick he uses to remind him to connect positively with his huggers. Each morning, he sticks ten pennies in his left pocket. Whenever he compliments or otherwise hugs an associate, he shifts a penny to his right pocket. When he empties his pockets at night, his goal is that all ten will have traveled to the right pocket. That way, he makes sure to fit in at least ten hugs a day.

When Todd told me about this, I loved the idea and started doing it myself, and I also urged all of our associates to try the penny habit to show that they notice and appreciate their colleagues. All it takes is a dime and the time. And I've got nothing against shooting for a quarter or a half-dollar!

Connecting can happen in a zillion ways. For instance, calling people by their nicknames. The fact that you know the nickname shows that you've personalized the relationship. Using it shows that you're thoughtful. Another easy yet powerful connection is to walk around the store or stand at the door after a busy day and, as associates leave, simply say, "Thank you, Jennifer, thank you, Rosa Lee," using the person's name or nickname.

I send personalized handwritten birthday and store anniversary cards to all our associates—including my sons and the family members who work with us. Each one is individually handwritten and signed with a real ink pen. People have said, "Sounds like a lot of work," but I don't find it to be a chore. I view it as a privilege. Fun really. For example, I wrote John Hickey III on his fiftieth birthday: "I'm thinking about you . . . it's nifty to be fifty . . . you are in the best shape . . . inner and outer game as you pass this big day." He mentioned to me with a chuckle, "Thanks, and I was absolutely thrilled." And to some of our sixty-year-old senior associates like myself, I might add, "It's sexy to be sixty!"

You can connect in so many ways. When Allison Borowy, Todd Mitchell's assistant, was working from home for two weeks while recovering from surgery, Todd arranged for Greg from our shipping department to hand deliver a Starbucks coffee to her (this was at the height of her addiction to caramel macchiatos). He was connecting.

Bill Mitchell is so avid about writing postcards of appreciation that he even scribbles them while on vacation. And when he returns he makes a habit of bringing in flowers—he seems to do it practically every day—and presenting them to a lucky person. He adores massages—he probably gets one at least once a week—and he knows that certain associates like to get their backs rubbed, too, so every now and then he hands them a certificate for a massage. Once Bill took the entire shipping and receiving department to a UConn basketball game, because they were big fans. And, you know what, the next time we had to ask them to deliver some suits at five o'clock on a Friday, instead of getting grumpy excuses like others might give, they said, "Sure, be happy to," and they did it with a smile. It's not why you make these connections, but it's not a bad residual benefit.

At a Mitchell family council meeting a few years ago, we were asked to draw a name out of a hat and do something special for this person in secret, not a random act of kindness but a proactive hug. I happened to pick Bill's name and I had flowers sent to his home every day (I thought it might cause more of a stir if I had them sent to the store from a "secret friend"). It got to the point where Bill actually came to me and said, "Do you know who is sending me these flowers? Because my wife is getting a little jealous" (which, by the way, he quickly said was good for his marriage).

IT DOESN'T HAVE TO BE A BEAR HUG

A bear hug, of course, is in many ways the best human connection. Before writing *Hug Your Customers*, I confess I was not a natural-born bear hugger like Bill. But since the book, many, many people have come up to me and said, with open arms, "I need a hug." And you know what? I learned to love giving and receiving hugs. If you know the person is not a bear hugger, fine, a firm handshake works just great. Since I'm an old jock, I like high fives, and I usually get a joyful smirk, especially from those who may have played basketball or baseball or have a daughter or son who plays a team sport. The high five makes them feel like part of the team.

Now, I've heard a few people say they're a little reluctant to physically hug an associate out of worry about sexual harassment laws. "Jack," a friend of mine from a prestigious banking firm said to me over dinner, "we tell our associates to never, ever bear hug, because we might be sued."

"Sad," I replied. "Very, very sad, Tom."

I know it's a challenge. It's a real shame in many ways that the government has imposed so many rules and regulations that inhibit the human connection. A balance needs to be struck. If you have a rule that says you can't literally hug someone, as is true at some businesses, it discourages a lot of personal bonding. The point is to know your audience. You should give a physical hug only when you've established a personal relationship and have a good sense of how the hug will be received by the hugee.

As Robin Imbrogno, president of the Human Resources Group, says, "Anyone can also feel harassed by a verbal or non-verbal statement. Telling someone they 'look good' can be just as easily construed as sexual harassment as a hug—it is the delivery, the intent, and the perception that could make it harassing or perceived as harassing."

So it's always important to get a good reading on the person. Tony at Marshs always reminds me that a hug in Italian is a "kiss," and so we always "hug" with a gentle kiss on the cheek. But I don't try that with strangers.

Let's be abundantly clear: you don't have to physically hug. Most hugs are very straightforward and wonderful—something as simple as a warm, friendly, embracing comment or two about a person, such as, "Wow, what a great tie" or "Those earrings are gorgeous." We belong to an organization of stores around the world that we call the IMG (International Menswear

Group). Oger Lusink, a new member from Holland, is a super hugger, and he began a great tradition. Every time he enters one of his stores, he shakes hands and looks each associate in the eye. Now all of his associates do the same thing—shake hands and look one another in the eye—every day.

I love this idea. I can understand how it's not for everyone. Some may feel it's too "forced" and thus phony. But Oger is consistent and genuine, and I believe that you need regular handshakes or friendly greetings to enhance a productive, powerful, passionate, personalized culture. Bill reminds me that it's just like how the UConn women's basketball team huddles up after every foul, reinforcing the human connection.

When you connect with someone, you often see an immediate impact. I'll always remember Joe D'Eufemia coming to me and in a warm way thanking me for sending him a card marking his tenth anniversary with us, and for the words I wrote. Joe's eyes filled with tears when he told me that when he went to bed the previous night he left the card on his bedside table and his wife saw it. When she read it, she was blown away by the appreciation.

Joe had worked for another employer for more than twenty years. He shared with me, "My boss never said boo to me. No one had ever sent me a birthday card, let alone an anniversary card! And now my wife—and this was the big hug, Jack—finally realized how much I've done for others in the store and how respected I truly am by my colleagues and customers for being, as you said, 'one of the best sales associates in the country.' "

A few years ago, I was on vacation and I left voice-mail messages for a couple of sales associates, injecting little personal flourishes into each one. Not long ago, Joe Cox came over to me and said, "When I get down and discouraged, I listen to your voice-mail message that I've kept for years. It makes me feel good all over again." That really blew me away!

He went and called his phone and let me eavesdrop. "See, I can start every day with you, and I know I've got a friend," he said. "Makes me feel appreciated."

Connections shouldn't just be top down, but also sideways and bottom up. For instance, when Sandra Nacewicz sent me a birthday card with a handwritten note and a donation to the Yale Cancer Center in Mom's name, I knew she went the extra mile and took the time to find out what charity would be important to me. You see, I'm on the Advisory Board at Yale and Mom died of breast cancer. Sandra connected with me in a personal manner; it was a very nice thing to do.

MAKE OUTSOURCERS FEEL LIKE INSIDERS

Today, a lot of activities are outsourced—for instance, we outsource human resources, security, store maintenance, and landscaping. Companies tend to treat outsourced people as second-tier and not really part of the team. That's nonsense. You have to connect with them in the same way you do with all your associates. I send birthday and anniversary cards to them, as well.

As Robin Imbrogno, our human resources leader, told me, "There are so many little things that your associates do to make us feel part of the team, like Gerry or Angela offering Theresa a ride home when they hear she's missed her train, or Regina and Melissa and the Richards team singing happy birthday on her birthday. When Pam Madonia was in a car accident, many cards and flowers and calls came to her home to see how she was doing. I've never, ever been made to feel like an outsider—and sometimes other companies do make me feel that way."

The same philosophy goes for people geographically removed from our stores. All of our men's special orders go through Evelyn Shelton, a wonderful hugger who now lives in Atlanta but comes up for trunk shows. Sara Lee, our full-time programmer, lives in California. They get hugged regularly, because they deserve it.

KEEP THOSE POSITIVE WORDS COMING

Choice of word is critical when you connect. Saying *associate*, rather than *help, clerk,* or even *employee,* clearly elevates the position in our staff's and other people's eyes. *Employee* and *employer* always sound so cold to me. We are all employees, even me. I like to think I'm an associate as well as an owner.

My ears pick up negative vibes when I hear—and I hear it a lot—"Jack, may I be honest with you?" Or "Honestly, I want to share . . ." It sounds as if you are not honest most of the time, or maybe all of the time. I substitute the word *candid:* "Let me be candid with you," rather than "Let me be honest with you." It makes all the difference.

Another one that really gets to me is when I say, "How are you today?" and someone says, "I'm great!" What they really mean, of course, is that they feel great. Otherwise it comes across as bragging. In a humble Niceness Culture, "I am great" just doesn't fly. On the other hand, for a long time I've used *great* to introduce individuals that I'm bragging about, or as a compliment, such as the great Bruce Lagerfeldt, the great Ellen Ndini, the great Taffy Parisi, the great Beverly Martin. Again, it has to be genuine, and it is. Beverly, for example, has given me feedback about how she loves being introduced that way.

I've even created a grid of what we think of as the leading positive words and phrases, along with the most negative ones. It's amazing how people light up when you speak in "positive language."

Top Five Positive Words	Negative Words
Challenge or opportunity	Problem
Associate or hugger	Employee, worker, or help
Standards, expectations, principles, or guidelines	Rules or regulations
Education	Training
Projects and programs	Chores, jobs, tasks

Top Five Positive Phrases	Negative Phrases
I need your help	That's not my job, or I'm busy
Let me be candid	Let me be honest
I *feel* great	I *am* great
I like this, *and*	I like this, *but*
What do you think?	I'll do it all myself

It also helps a lot if you "speak their language"—literally. For example, I try to at least say "Good morning" in Spanish,

Greek, and Italian to those associates who speak those languages.

Body language can be every bit as meaningful as spoken language, and everyone needs to take a hard look at his or her own body language. Standing with your arms folded, for instance, is a defensive posture that to me says, "Stay away," and I avoid it, even if I'm chilly. I've been told that I don't look people in the eyes enough, and so I've worked hard to correct that. For some reason, I used to nod the wrong way—a terrible habit I somehow picked up—so that if I agreed with you I would nod left to right rather than up and down. I was agreeing with you but you would think I was disagreeing. And so I've consciously practiced to shake the habit, and I've pretty much gotten it licked.

WHAT IF THEY DON'T HUG?

For most of our associates, hugging comes naturally and so they're constantly connecting with one another, but not always. We're often asked, "How do you get a manager or associate to hug if they aren't hugging?"

There are only two reasons they don't hug:

1. They don't know how to: If they don't know how to hug but they demonstrate they are willing to learn, we are extremely patient. We influence by example and by pointing out positive behaviors of other teammates as well as negative, non-hugging behavior. And we celebrate each and every little hug we see them giving. Sooner or later, the lightbulb goes on and he or she gets it and finds ways to hug all the time.

2. They don't want to: If this is the case, and they are candid enough to say so or continue to act the same way, then they have to go. Actually, they generally resign, because they see that they're a bad fit culturally.

In our case, this rarely happens because associates have already gone through the hugging interview process. We know they desire to hug but in their past experiences they may lack one or two insights or skills to open up their hearts and souls to hugging.

It's like you need to practice a hundred layups before you make them all. Suppose everyone picks up merchandise for a colleague except you. You do it with the group and then one day you do it on your own. Not just to please someone else, though that's important, but you do it naturally because it's the appropriate thing to do. Plus—and here's the key part—you feel great. And someone will say, "Wow, thanks for the hug. You really have changed, you really care about me."

And you realize you are truly part of the Mitchells/Richards/Marshs hugging team.

CHAPTER 6

Work Is Play, It's Fun

You hear that tired old cliché all the time—don't mix business with pleasure. Well, it's so tired it needs to be retired. *Work* and *fun* shouldn't be considered antonyms. We think of them as synonyms.

When people are happy and having fun, they're much more productive. And it's an infectious feeling. Steve Anderson, a friend of mine who heads Total Patient Service, a consultant to dental practices, is a big proponent of happy associates, and he likes to share his beliefs on his Web site. He mentioned recently: "Scientists have discovered how quickly we adopt the emotional state of those around us by measuring the physiology, heart rate, blood pressure, skin temperature, et cetera, of two people sharing a conversation. As the conversation gets started, the vital signs of the two bodies are different. But after fifteen minutes, the physiological profiles of the two bodies become very similar." So there you have it, he says—scientific proof! One associate's happiness becomes the other associate's happiness.

And yet at many companies (how about yours?) associates often feel downright guilty if they're having a good time. You know the scenario: a cluster of associates are chuckling over something when the big boss arrives and everyone immediately adopts a somber face and scurries to their desk to look like they're "working." Colleen Kenny told me how a previous boss once told her: "No small talk during work hours. I don't care what you watched on TV last night. I don't care what joke you heard on Leno. I don't care what trick your dog learned. You're here to work."

Well, in a Niceness Culture the boss joins in the laughter. We want people to bring their real selves to work, not some artificial "business self." And so when I walked into Richards the other day about a half hour before the store officially opened, I loved it that associates were smiling and chuckling, and absolutely thrilled to see Rocco dancing with Edit. They love to dance. I felt like cutting in but instead started singing, and suddenly every-one around us was cheering and having fun. If you want to dance at work, dance! Sing, go for it, sing—as Oscar often encourages me to do when he says he thinks my singing is intoxicating.

The reason I always make a point of asking associates, espe-cially during an interview, "What do you do for fun?" is that I want to signal from the top that it's okay to have fun at work.

My colleague Pamela once said to me, "You know, Jack, many people say work is a four-letter word!" And I said back to her, "Work actually *is* a four-letter word, and the way you spell it is p-l-a-y."

I've always looked at work as play. When Linda says to me, "Jack, I've got some plans for you today, could you go outside and dig up twenty-five holes for the trees and flowers I want to plant," well, that's work! I'll do it, because I love Linda, but I'd rather be playing tennis or, better yet, going to Mitchells.

Because we want people to have fun at work, our managers are always looking for new ways to do just that. Once, led by poker enthusiast Todd Mitchell, we invited our associates to the store for an evening of Texas hold 'em, the hottest game in poker. It was loads of fun, won in fact by Jill Olson, who had never before played the game. Several brand-new associates attended and it sent a big message to them. For one thing, it demonstrated that everyone plays on an equal playing field and that we are fashionable in the way that we hug all our huggers. Best of all, it showed that we like to have fun together.

When we first merged with Richards, we hired a bus and went to Foxwoods Resort and Casino, playing cards all the way up and back, and when we got there we had dinner and gambled. There was great bonding, hugging, and lots of laughter. Some of us even won a few bucks.

I even heard that some people went up on the bus with us, but they took their $25 gambling voucher we had given them and instead had a nice Italian dinner, got to know one another a little bit more, and had a ton of fun!

Don't get the wrong idea: we're not all one step away from Gamblers Anonymous. We have a good time in myriad ways.

One day, a bunch of our sellers and buyers, and a few others, visited with some executives from Ermenegildo Zegna at their New York showrooms to get an overview of the spring collection. Afterward everyone, including the Zegna folks, went bowling. Zegna outfitted us with colorful T-shirts and we filled ten lanes. Everyone learned a lot and everyone had great fun. Bill likes to say, "Bowling is the great equalizer." And it sure was that day. It was such a hoot that the other night Chris Mitchell invited all the associates at Marshs out to the lanes and continued the bowling spirit!

I love to play games with words and letters, and I regularly invite others to join in. The basic idea is to come up with positive words. We'll have a meeting and I'll say, "Let's try to think of positive words that start with *P*." And people will volunteer words: *profit, praise, pride*. My favorites, of course, are my new three *P*'s: *positive, passionate,* and *personalization*. We'll write them down—sometimes there are dozens—and then share them in my CEO letter that goes out to everyone. Then I'll ask for more words. Then I'll ask for stories behind *pride* or behind *passion*. The whole thing has really caught on. Once we exhaust one letter, we move on and do it with others.

I call it the Power of Positive Words.

What's great about this game is that using positive words has a very intoxicating effect. Positive words will stick in people's subconscious and they'll find themselves using them when they interact with one another.

Almost every Saturday morning at the Richards women associates meetings, run by Scott Mitchell, my nephew, he'll kick things off by dreaming up questions like "What is one word that describes you?" Or "If your great-aunt died and left you more money than Bill Gates, what would you do with it?"

Then he'll go around and let people answer. It's a really fun exchange, and it's amazing what you can learn about your colleagues. For the money question, it was nice to hear that most said they would give a lot of the money away to improve the world. The best part of this game is that it temporarily extracts the "business" from the meeting and injects a nice warm atmosphere of sharing, personalizing relationships among the huggers.

FOLLOW MR. FUN

Bob Mitchell, my son, is known at our stores as Mr. Fun, because he's always "preaching" about the importance of fun. He incorporates the thought whenever he addresses a meeting. In the beginning, the middle, and at the end of any discussion, he makes a point of weaving in the message "Let's have fun doing this."

The more urgent or serious the discussion, the more crucial it is to remind people to have fun. So he might be winding up a talk about pumping up sales and urging everyone, "Let's all make twenty customer calls today," and then immediately soften that with, "And let's have fun doing it."

And he likes to jump up and down when he says it to really drive home the point.

When voice mail first came about, my son Russell began to personalize his outgoing message with the date and his location. I copied the idea, and updated my message each day with what store I was going to be at, or when I was out and when I would return. But I've gone the next step and always try to give my message a little enthusiasm and energy, and maybe even a little something like, "Come down and see me in Timbuktu." When associates leave messages for me, I often hear them chuckling in the background. I imagine they're thinking, "What an upbeat and unusual message!"

You can also spice things up with fun challenges. Not long ago, Trish and Claire decided it was time to shed some winter weight. And so they wanted to have some fun with that. They announced a weigh-in. Everyone would contribute a modest sum to a pool and whoever achieved the largest percentage weight loss over a month's time would claim the money—and hopefully not use it to go out for a six-course meal.

I love the story about Jack Kahl, when he was president of Manco, the duct tape maker that's now part of the Henkel Group. He began an annual challenge that if the sales force hit its target, he would swim the width of the duck pond outside the company's Ohio headquarters—and do it on a brisk day to boot. If the salespeople came up short, then they had to plunge into the water. Jack did the swim the first year, and didn't mind it one bit. He was having fun, and so was everyone else.

So go for it!

Work is play.

So go play today!

Have fun!

CHAPTER 7

Not Everyone Wants an Orchid

Hugs sometimes backfire, even the best-intentioned ones. And when a hug goes awry, it becomes a slap in the face, the exact opposite of what was intended.

Hugs generally miss when you don't know the person you want to hug well enough. A friend of mine told me about a boss who gave one of his colleagues a bottle of champagne. Sounds like a very thoughtful gift—especially since it was a top brand—except that the person was a recovering alcoholic. Occasionally this happens. Of course, the recipient may graciously accept the bottle of liquor, but it's not the hug a pair of tickets to *American Idol* would have been.

After all, as I once kidded Pamela, who is a vegetarian, what kind of a hug would it be if I took her out for a steak dinner? Or how do you think a very good friend of mine, who is kosher, feels when you serve him shrimp or pork?

It's not really that these things are wrong, because they are intended as kind, hugging gestures, but they certainly demonstrate that the giver really doesn't "know" the person.

Most of the time, you don't know when a hug doesn't work, because the recipient rarely says anything, for fear of being rude. I dare say that the boss who gave the champagne still doesn't know that his colleague is a teetotaler.

But if you have a culture that fosters candid feedback, then associates will either directly or indirectly let you know if the hugs you give are wide of the mark. And I expect they'll do so politely, and with a smile. And no offense will be taken.

A good example of this process occurred during a recent holiday season, a time of year when we like to send flowers to some of our very best friends and customers. We used to give poinsettia plants with a personal note from Bill or myself. Indeed, some of them we called whoppers, because they were practically trees. We got nice hugs back, in the form of thank-you cards, but then we began to listen more carefully to some people, who candidly shared with us that poinsettias are Christian symbols of Christ.

The next year, we switched to cyclamen and later to orchids, which we continue to favor. And almost to the person we receive very positive feedback. However, there are a few recipients who prefer that we not send them over the holidays while they are away or that we route them to a hospital or another "home" where they can be enjoyed. And then Art told us, "I don't like flowers and neither does my wife."

So I said, "What do you like?"

And he said, "I like cheesecake, I like pickles, I like blackberry jam."

So I sent him cheesecake, pickles, and blackberry jam. Simple as that. And now he and his wife couldn't be happier.

To make sure that the people who like roses get roses and the people who like pickles get pickles, we make a point of always encouraging feedback. And we try hard to be alert to feeble or nonexistent thanks. If you send something meaningful to a valued associate and all you get in return is a limp expression of gratitude, or none at all, that's a sure tip-off that the hug may have flopped.

In a positive way, find out why. Ask. And preferably do it face-to-face, eyeball to eyeball. Then acknowledge the miscue, fix it, and finish up by giving the person an extra hug—some pickles, say, plus theater tickets if they would like to see a Broadway show.

CHAPTER 8

Now That You've Connected, Reconnect

It's a terrific, warm feeling when you connect with someone in the personal ways I spoke about earlier. But you have to sustain that connection, or it quickly loses its oomph. That means that you have to *reconnect*.

Reconnect is an exercise that we learned for our family business from David Bork, my friend and a top-notch family business consultant. David has been working with us for almost twenty-five years, through three generations and now onto the fourth. We first used this technique at family council sessions when all the Mitchells and their spouses and partners gather together. Without fail, we begin every council meeting with it and I've found it's helpful for our other meetings, as well as for more informal and spontaneous encounters, like when you bump into someone on the elevator or at the water cooler.

Here's how it works. Suppose you're having a meeting.

Number one on the agenda is "Reconnect." Before you get to the business at hand, go around the room and, depending on time restraints and how long it's been since you've seen them, give each participant one to five minutes of uninterrupted time to share with everyone else what's on his or her mind. If I'm chairing the meeting, I often will go first to get it going and then simply move around the table and say, "What's going on with you? What's happened lately?"

In fact, as Margret McBride, my literary agent, points out about reconnecting, "Sharing can be awkward for some people at first. Let others go first so they get the idea. When everyone can participate in an open way, relationships are created—some last a lifetime!"

In the beginning, you should emphasize that it would be great if they say something personal as well as something about business, but leave it entirely up to them.

Essentially, it's a matter of "Tell me what and how you've been doing since the last time I saw you." Even if that was yesterday.

The answers will range all over the place, as they should. You'll hear that Cathy Kozak's daughter is going to college. David bought a house. Marilyn read a great novel. Robert learned his first child will be a girl. Frank lost twenty-nine pounds.

Sometimes, Scott Mitchell asks a slightly offbeat question to get people reconnecting. One of my favorites is: "What is something that no one knows about you?" At one meeting, Beverly revealed that for some strange reason she really likes to do the dishes in the dark. That got all of us laughing and thinking.

When you try this exercise, it's important not to pry—when

Frank mentions he lost weight you don't have to grill him to find out his current weight. Let people mention what they want, and leave it at that. In fact, the less you pry the more the quiet, private people will eventually open up.

And you do have to be willing to let people pass. When they schedule meetings, a lot of businesses send out notices beforehand that stress, "Everyone come prepared to say something." That's absolutely the wrong way to do it. Then everyone feels stressed or put on the spot. You have to be allowed to say nothing, even if you're senior management. Some people are bashful, some people might be in a foul mood that day, some people might be distracted that day. It's all okay. And it must be made clear that not participating won't be held against you. It won't go in your file with red flags scribbled all over it (which indeed does happen at many businesses).

After all, for some people it takes time to be comfortable in an open, hugging environment; others will rattle on and tell you everything about their weekend—the good, the bad, the ugly, the top hundred basketball scores—far more information than you want. That's why you impose a time limit.

The whole point of this exercise is that you're perpetuating the human connection. We believe it brings everyone back to common ground. It's important to realize that a Niceness Culture means keeping in touch with your total life, not just your career at work but your entire journey through life. Reconnecting is a reminder that we care about you and eventually you will care about us.

Indeed, once relationships become truly personalized,

people really open up when they reconnect. In her reconnect at a recent meeting, Sally shared how her daughter was doing. She had had enormous emotional and substance abuse challenges in high school and had spent a month in detox before enrolling in boarding school. And later in the meeting we were talking about anniversary dates and Sally said, "All right, I have to share that today is my two-year anniversary of sobriety." Everyone congratulated her and she said she felt warm inside.

Even Warren Buffett indulges in this exercise at his stockholder meetings. Although I've never attended a Buffett picnic, I know that he and his alter ego sit up there and chat and answer questions in a casual manner—they're reconnecting with their multitude of stockholders!

By reconnecting, listening, and storing information about someone, you can discover things that can help associates in their work. I remember interviewing a young woman with Beverly Martin, the assistant manager of women's clothing, and it was clear that she was a shy person. She was hired and I mentioned her shyness months later when I was reconnecting with her, and she said, "No Jack, I'm just reserved."

I chuckled and said, "I like *reserved* better, because it's tough to be a seller and be shy."

When we were doing her review later that year, I asked her to share with us a story of when she's not reserved. She said she wasn't bashful when she boomed out gospel songs in church.

Fast-forward a few months. Her sales were weak. Recalling what she had mentioned, Bev and I reminded her of what she had said during her review and we challenged her to be positive and step up, she had to get up and belt out those solos like she did at church.

And boy did she ever turn up the volume! And Beverly, in a caring and compassionate way, coached her and guided her to success.

Reconnecting is a form of communication between people. It can be one-on-one, although the reconnecting exercise from our David Bork roots is mostly done in a group setting. Communication that allows for reconnecting occurs in at least four ways, and I'll list them in order of warmness preference:

1. In person, either one-on-one or in group meetings
2. Telephone or video conferencing
3. Notes or letters
4. E-mail

Our advice: use them all!

And we strongly believe that in face-to-face encounters at least the first minute and the last minute of the reconnect should be personal. The same goes for the beginning and closing of an e-mail or letter. The message softens and makes the recipient feel better when the e-mail or note says, "Dear Michele, how was the shore?" Or "Dear Sarah, how was your daughter's first year in college?" Or "Hope to see you soon, great talking with you, give my best to Lynn." Something you would say if you were looking them straight in the eye.

I also try to start a letter or e-mail with the word "you." For example, I began a recent e-mail, "You've been on my mind all day . . ." Many times, I'll finish an e-mail and realize I was being impersonal and I'll go back and revise the first sentence so it sounds as if I were talking to the person.

In between the beginning and the end of the communication, of course, you need to do business. But that personal opening and ending underscore the fact that business is about relationships. The "Dear" in the beginning and "Hope to see you soon" at the end—those are hugs, and they'll be appreciated. I also like the Jack Welch idea of keeping any written letter to one page or even a note card—suitable for framing later. Bill and I each have a framed note card from Jack.

So saunter down the hall right now and try to Reconnect. See how Todd Bonner's daughter is doing with her NASTAR skiing or how Kathleen Mitchell is doing with her violin lessons. Find out how Derrick's wife is faring with her chemo. Ask Todd how his son Ryan's swimming lessons are going. Or see how Stanley is coping with his new artificial knee and ask when he can resume sailing.

Of course, so many of you do this in an informal way with your family and friends. I'm sure there are many examples in business. Hopefully, the process that I've shared may give you a new idea or two to use. Once you get the real hang of reconnecting, you'll realize, Wow, this is a nice thing to do, and it will become a permanent part not only of your meeting agenda but also of your routine in life.

Being interested in others on a personalized basis becomes its own reward.

HUGGING STUDY GUIDE #1

NICE

Create a Niceness Culture: For associates to feel happy and motivated, you need a strategy to create a culture in which there's a "pleaser" mentality, relationships are positive and personalized with passion, and there is company-wide humility.

Hire nice people: Hire people who are competent and confident; positive; have the passion to learn, listen, and grow; and have integrity—and especially people who are nice. How do you tell? Would you like to sit next to them on a cross-country or around-the-world flight?

Become married for life: Forget about probationary periods and create an upbeat environment so new associates feel welcome and comfortable in your culture. Send flowers when they start, and perhaps even give them a small surprise cash bonus in the first six months.

Know their names and hobbies: Managers should know the names and something about their top 100 to 150 associates, if not the top 250: the person you report to, those who report to you, and those associates who make a difference in enabling you to deliver whatever you need to do to achieve your goals.

Connect: Hug associates in myriad little ways tailored to their tastes and likes, and do it in a genuine and consistent manner. Smile, say thanks, pay for a car wash every once in a while.

Have fun: Business and pleasure do mix and are connected, so encourage your associates to laugh and have fun. Play the positive word game or poker. Go to work to play the game.

Fix the hugs that backfire: Not all hugs work—giving a bottle of liquor to a recovering alcoholic or candy to a diabetic is like a slap, so be alert to signs that a hug has backfired. Fix it with a smile and a fresh hug, plus an extra one for good measure.

Reconnect: Reinforce that personal bond by starting meetings or other encounters by asking associates to update everyone on what's been going on in their lives lately, and encourage them to be personal. Keep it short and sweet.

PART TWO

Trust

The Most Important Principle of All

CHAPTER 9

No Surprises

I remember when our son Andrew got involved in skydiving in New Zealand: thank God there was a parachute on his back—and one that could be trusted to open. When I take the grandkids to the beach, I trust that the lifeguards on duty will be on their toes and have quick reflexes to back me up. It's easy to understand why. In both instances, I'm talking about saving the lives of those very dear to me.

Trust is a big deal in all aspects of our lives, and a very big deal in the business world. No company flourishes for long without it.

If you think about it, trust is interchangeable with integrity. It is the foundation of all that we do for ourselves, our associates, our vendors, and our friends. We look at it as a continuum: we trust our associates, our associates trust us, we trust our customers, our customers trust us. And it's something that naturally grows out of our hugging culture and an environment built around niceness.

And if I had to choose, I'd say that trust is the most important principle of all. Without it, you don't really have anything. Studies of sports teams demonstrate that those where the players completely trust their coach tend to be the ones that are the most successful. Well, we think the same is true on the business playing field.

Trust is very much a hot-button issue today, in part because of all the intrusive technology that exists in our modern world. Employees feel degrees of stress and paranoia that they didn't before, because they hear that supervisors sometimes monitor phone calls with customers, are able to review private e-mail, and can even capture what someone does on his or her computer.

These matters are significant because the bond of trust is fragile. It's a lot easier to lose than create. All it takes is one lie to destroy the trust that millions of truths have established. As Warren Buffett once phrased it, "Trust is like the air we breathe. When it's present, nobody really notices. But when it's absent, everybody notices."

So what do you do to make people feel trusted?

It really comes down to the question, How do you educate others to always tell the truth? The answer for us is that you actively *promote* integrity. To me, the first and most important way is to live an honest life, for that becomes an example for others.

Now, I'm not saying I'm a saint. I do make mistakes. And so I believe it's very important not to punish people for the kind of

honest mistakes that everyone makes. A culture in which people fear mistakes leads to subterfuge.

In our hugging culture, when someone has "failed"—or
what we prefer to think of as done less than we or he hoped
for—the "mistakes" are honestly fixed with a smile. If you make
an error and are able to go to the boss or any teammate and say,
"I made a mistake and here's how I am going to recover," well,
providing an environment that fosters such openness is a hug
for your huggers.

I had an entire section called "I Love Mistakes" in *Hug Your
Customers*. Many readers e-mailed me to say that it was so re-
freshing to read about a culture where you acknowledge mistakes (and even at times practically celebrate them) so you can
learn from them and go forward.

In a trusting environment, when someone makes a mistake
and another associate brings it to his attention, it's seen as assistance, not a put-down. It's understood that honest feedback
is meant to help this person grow and hopefully avoid future
misunderstandings or similar mistakes.

Being consistent in what you say and do is important and
connected with trust. Inconsistent behavior and answers are
quick ways to erode trust. If you're inconsistent, then you're
contradicting yourself. You become two people. How does anyone know which one of your two selves to believe?

Every week, there are incidents that make me realize that we
come to the store with the attitude that we trust everyone, even
new people, who may be used to an environment where they
had to embellish the truth to get ahead and to make their

mark. The way we look at it, *trust really means there are no surprises.* In other words, there are no hidden agendas, no hidden half-truths, no cover-ups. No reason not to be forthright and candid all the time.

One simple method Linda and I learned a long time ago by raising four sons is that they don't have to tell you everything—and maybe it's best if they don't tell you *everything*—but when they do tell you something it had better be the truth. And it's still that way today.

As Bill likes to say, "It's a lot easier to remember the truth."

To take a small example, I don't believe in instructing secretaries or assistants to tell someone who calls that I'm in a meeting if I'm actually reviewing a report or practicing my putting stroke. Lying, even when it's a small white lie, is not a hug. If you're in a meeting, fine, but if you're not, say what you're doing, don't make it up. If associates can't trust you on the little things, they're certainly not going to trust you on the big things. You see this in courtrooms all the time. The opposing lawyer establishes that you fibbed about not liking pound cake—he's got actual videotape of you eating pound cake at the diner—and he tells the jury, "See, how can you trust anything this guy says?"

If there are going to be no surprises, then the associates need to be hugged by their leaders in a way so that there is no question in their minds about any detail. It boils down to meaning what you say. So if I ask someone to deliver a suit by Tuesday, that means the customer really needs it by Tuesday. It has to be altered by Tuesday morning and delivered by courier by Tuesday afternoon.

No surprises means that if I say you are going to get a bonus when you achieve a certain level of performance, then you get it on time, with a smile and a thank-you. It means knowing that the owners follow all of the government rules and don't cheat on their taxes, compensation, or hiring practices.

In short, it means you always tell the truth. Always, always, always.

CHAPTER 10

Have Expectations and Standards, Not Rules and Regulations

I'm told that many, even most, companies maintain thick employee handbooks jam-packed with all shapes and types of rules—rules about when you come to work and when you leave, rules about how often you get a break, rules about coarse language, rules about penalties for defacing bulletin boards, rules about this, that, and everything, so many that even the person who wrote them couldn't possibly know them all. Every year or so, they make revisions to the handbook, usually sticking in still more rules but rarely, if ever, discarding or updating any of them to reflect a changing world. So you have a business drowning in rules that no one can remember, including the managers who dreamed them up.

In this regard, companies are as bad as governments. I'm always reminded of this when I read about some antiquated local or state law that never got updated for common sense. For instance, South Carolina has a two-hundred-year-old law banning games with cards or dice—even in your own home. So I guess the police can bust in and haul you and the kids to the pen for playing Monopoly or Go Fish!

When you have piles of rules, we believe it makes people extremely uneasy. They feel like they're back in school—or, worse, in prison. And the upshot is that they don't feel as if they're trusted. One of our sales associates shared how, at another company, she came to work one day despite having wrenched her back the previous night. She was in a fair amount of discomfort, but didn't want to miss a day. So between customers, she sat down to ease the pain. Her supervisor spotted her, stomped over, and barked: "Get up right now. You can't sit, because it sets a bad example. It's the rule."

You know the old saying "Rules are made to be broken." Well, we find that people look on rules as meaning that you're testing their integrity. Which translates to "I don't trust you." So one of the most important ways we show that we trust our people is by not having rules except those required by law.

Now, when we say that we don't have any other rules, we don't mean that we operate in complete anarchy—maybe a touch of organized chaos, but not anarchy. No business could be successful if it were run that way. People don't come and go as they please, they don't have limitless expense accounts, they don't come to work in bikinis.

You see, we're a hugging culture based on values and principles, not rules and regulations.

So how do we establish parameters? Rather than rules, we

have expectations. And if you have a company comprised of trustworthy people, setting examples and expectations works a lot better than rules.

What's the difference between rules and expectations? To our mind, rules are unbending. If the rule is that you have to take lunch from noon to one o'clock and you don't take it at that time, then you starve to death. So rules are rigid. To me, they're cold and impersonal.

Expectations, on the other hand, are warm, and they're flexible and freeing when they need to be. The clear understanding is that you are expected to live up to our expectations, and so you come in and leave when you are scheduled to, but you don't need a time clock to keep you honest. Expectations are mutually agreed upon—and they can be fulfilled in different ways by different people. No two individuals are completely alike in talent, strengths, motivation, or personality—everyone has plenty of quirks or weaknesses—so why should everyone have to follow rigid rules? Expectations are pliable and they may be adjusted to suit an individual and build on his or her strengths.

What, then, are some of our expectations?

There are seven key expectations that are important to me:

1. Be positive, passionate, and personal.
2. Work and play hard—and work smarter, too.
3. Understand the power of the team. That means exhibiting mutual respect and trust. Fun and success mean *we*,

not *I* (remember the old expression, "There is no 'I' in team").

4. Dress appropriately (this especially applies to us since we're in the clothing business).

5. No surprises.

6. Always, always be open and tell the truth!

7. Hug one another and hug the customers!

We also like to use the word *standards* a lot in place of *rules*. In general, we set very high standards, and we expect everyone to do their level best to live up to them. My tenth-grade civics teacher wrote in my Staples High School yearbook, "Live up to your potential," and I obviously never forgot it and think about it often, and that's what we want our people to do: live up to their highest potential.

That's why effort, hard work, and education are emphasized. We like people to keep raising the bar, especially in areas where they are naturally strong. We realize that if the bar is raised appropriately with each individual in mind, then everyone will reach his or her personal and professional goals and will enjoy—indeed love—the journey, the process, the playing of the game of the career of life.

And so within our expectations we establish specific standards, or targets. For instance, we expect our sellers to achieve $1 million in sales their first year with us (but we don't horsewhip them if they do $900,000). We expect tailors to be fast and accurate—we never like pants that end six inches above the ankle—and to work as a team. And, of course, we expect everyone to support one another in a sale, to share their skills and "secrets" on personalizing relationships with other huggers, and to store data for everyone to use in an open and honest way with respect for privacy and confidentiality.

So set expectations for your associates, but leave rules to the prison wardens.

CHAPTER 11

A New World Environment, the "Of Course" Philosophy

Not long ago when I was in Washington, D.C., I was picked up by an Ethiopian taxi driver. As we cruised past a group of protesters invoking their right to demonstrate in our nation's capital, the taxi driver shared with me that in his native country protesters "were often shot or imprisoned—like I was. Indeed, I still marvel at the American democratic system that encourages free speech and individual thought."

This unscripted exchange made me realize again how lucky we all are to live in a country where free speech and liberty are available to all.

The taxi story came to mind one day when I was speaking with Patricia at Richards. She said that when she joined us from a large retail chain she felt that she had "moved from a Third World country to a democracy." I probed a little, and Patricia said that the culture at the other store had been stifling at first, but that she had grudgingly gotten used to it and became resigned to it. She just assumed that all retail stores worked that way.

When she started with us, she said, "From day one, I was overwhelmed by the positive change in culture." She realized that she could speak her mind without fear of retribution. At her old company, associates were reluctant to speak up or to offer their own ideas, and few did.

"Here," Patricia said, "I have learned to be who I am—it's been like a caterpillar becoming a butterfly. Now I'm flying all over the store!"

I am so glad that we all embrace this democracy, making this flight together.

What's revealing about Patricia's story is the fact that after working at another big company in our industry she got used to "the country" and its culture. Like someone from the old communist Eastern Europe contemplating the wider world, she had figured that every place in retail and business was like that. She was positive, upbeat, and productive. Her company was a pretty good place to work. Customers were buying, she had benefits and decent pay—who was she to question that there was another way? Lo and behold, one or two people who had left told her, "We're working for a store in Greenwich called Richards. And, you won't believe it, it's very, very different. It's like coming to the New World."

Now we recognize that the hugging culture is not for everyone. Some folks actually prefer a dictatorship where they don't have to make any decisions or voice any opinions but are always told what to do. It's just the way they're built. But we believe most people that want to fly far and away favor the New World, because it means they are trusted and can be themselves. As Judy Brooks and Joe DeRosa say, "I can grow being me."

From our experience, accomplishing a true New World environment requires three crucial things:

1. There is freedom with responsibility.

Freedom is obviously a big word and a big concept, and it's the underpinning of a New World environment. But freedom is not entirely free.

Heidi Williams is a good illustration. She's been with us for almost fifteen years, and is just a wonderful person. Over this period, she has had some personal illness and some family health issues that have meant a fair amount of time away from the store. It's a big deal to her personally and to us as well, since we care about Heidi and she is a powerful and productive sales associate at Mitchells. She's been very appreciative of how we've all—not only our family but her fellow associates, who have pinch-hit for her and communicated with customers to keep them apprised of Heidi's progress and to keep them loyal and happy—hugged her during these times and granted her the freedom to deal with her challenges.

At the same time, no one could have been more responsible than Heidi was in handling these challenges. At times, she worked from home, signing letters and making appointments for other associates. She regularly called and spoke to Todd Mitchell, who manages the women's business at Mitchells. And the minute she had the health and strength to come in and work for a few hours, and eventually a full day, she did. And now we're delighted that she's back on a permanent, full-time basis.

I think it was Thomas Jefferson who said something like "the flip side of freedom is responsibility." And I say, and I'm certainly not Jefferson, that the foundation of freedom and responsibility is trust. Thomas Jefferson would have been as proud of Heidi as we were!

The key is she understood that you can't abuse freedom. You earn it through responsibility. And this adds up to trust.

It's important that you trust people on the little things, because they matter more than you think. For instance, a lot of businesses have dumb restrictions, such as codes that associates have to punch in to use the copiers. We don't do that. It sends the message that associates aren't trusted and it seems chintzy as well. It smacks of thinking of associates as expenses rather than assets. A lot of people I speak to on airplanes and in supermarkets and brokerage houses feel as if they are just a number and expense, rather than assets paying dividends for their company.

2. No one is forced to do anything.

In the end, you really only do what you want to do. When you're forced to do something, you may do nothing more than go through the motions, and in the long run that's counter to our culture. What's consistent with our culture is to explain the *value* of why we believe satisfaction calls are important, and why it's crucial to double-check everything in the tailor shop, and why it's important and fun to come to a company picnic. Rather than force people, we are more than willing to discuss why a particular individual might do a particular task or participate in a particular event, and many times there is a good reason that is acceptable to everyone.

I hear that in other cultures people are sometimes forced to attend meetings or seminars or social functions, events where they have to sip cocktails and schmooze with people they don't know because "it helps drive the business numbers." Which means, of course, that many times money outweighs their personal lives or feelings.

The classic example is when you are forced to go to a meeting, finish a project, or travel halfway around the world to Bahrain while your spouse, child, or grandchild is celebrating a birthday or graduating or has a big field hockey game—and you had to miss it. You know it happens a lot!

Not only do you not enjoy your assignment, or enjoy the event or project that takes you away, but also you often don't agree with the purpose of it because you were not part of the decision-making process. Your participation and sense of engagement were taken for granted. You were never told how valuable you are and why it was you and not anyone else chosen for this important job. And so your mind—and heart—are somewhere else.

George Kanganis, a world-class hugger and the national sales manager for FTD Group, Inc., told me about having to send one of his guys away on a trip when it was his son's fifth birthday. "I regret it and will never do that again!" George exclaimed. "It went against my grain to ask someone to be away from home when there is an important family event." We're the same way.

This is where personalizing relationships comes in big-time. When an associate has a pressing reason to take time off and they don't have a personal relationship with their manager, they often feel forced to lie, or at least not tell the full truth, saying they are sick or their hamster is giving birth to get the time off.

Do you really want people to have tension at work, and never feel a personal connection and involvement for life? Talk about establishing loyalty!

And when something needs to be done, it makes such a difference to ask someone by saying, "Would you please," rather than brusquely saying, "Do it."

The best way to enlist people to do things is to do them right alongside them. Doreen Nugent in accounts payable likes to tell about one Christmas season when the store was mobbed and customer service was shorthanded. Russ Mitchell asked her if she would come down and help out. She was leery. She had never rung up a purchase and hadn't wrapped a gift since the Reagan years.

But when she got downstairs, Russ immediately thanked her for pitching in and set her up at the gift-wrap station. Meanwhile, she was mightily impressed that *he* rang up sales, wrapped gifts, and rode out that wave of Christmas madness alongside everyone else.

In the end, she loved helping out. Russ even taught her the secret to her all-time biggest fear: how to fold, box, and wrap a winter coat.

From that day forward, she realized the difference between working *for* someone and working *with* someone as part of his team. The whole experience gave her a deeper understanding of how the business worked, as well as helped her to forge relationships with associates that she might otherwise not have had the opportunity to work with. All by being asked, not forced.

3. The answer is "Of course." Not long ago, I was interviewing an associate from another retailer for a job at Marshs. This was her second interview, after being seen by Bob and my nephew Chris Mitchell. She said, "You guys have to stop, you have no comprehension. You all are happy. It sounds like everyone wants to go to work and that you have a *yes culture*. Most of the people where I work don't want to go to work and they have a *no culture*. Every time I come up with an idea they say no."

We find it's a lot more enjoyable to say yes, and so we do. All the time.

At a previous employer, Sally had become close friends with a person who worked in her department. Sadly, her friend's father died. Sally asked to leave early on a Friday afternoon to go to the four p.m. funeral. She had arranged for coverage. Her supervisor, more concerned with "substitute-coverage" than personal loss, said no. Both she and her friend were crushed. Sally had never asked for time off or taken a sick day. It was not a coincidence that within a month they had both transferred to other departments. Had the supervisor been more compassionate, they might still be working there.

I heard a story about a group of associates who were

assembled for a meeting with the new director of their team. He wondered aloud why the team was behind schedule, and asked what he could do to galvanize things. One person spoke up and said it would be nice to have a refrigerator in the conference room stocked with Pepsi. A couple hours later, a mini-fridge materialized in the room crammed with Pepsi, Diet Pepsi, and Aquafina. Some cold soda doesn't seem like a big deal, but it told everyone that the new guy listened and cared and it perked everyone up. Soon enough, everything was on time again. That's a yes culture.

When I speak to other companies about our hugging philosophy, I do a routine where I explain how we are an Of Course Culture. Of course we will help people in need. Of course we will visit them in the hospital. Of course we will have a holiday party. Of course we will have free coffee, tea, and sparkling water for our associates. Of course we will have birthday cakes and celebrate anniversaries. Of course, of course, of course!

Associates love hearing it.

And we feel great saying it.

And of course we enjoy doing it!

CHAPTER 12

We Like Things Transparent

All the time, our new associates tell us that at the last place they worked they really were mostly in the dark about the fortunes of the company. All they heard was sell more, more, more. Work harder, harder, harder. Numbers, numbers, numbers. And yet they often didn't even know if they were ahead of or behind the previous year. By working harder, they didn't understand what they were accomplishing.

In fact, often the only time they knew how things were going was when they picked up *The Wall Street Journal* and found out that sales were tanking and five operations were being closed, including theirs—today!

Or, wow, they had a great quarter, yet no one seemed to be celebrating.

And if they wanted to see the big boss about something

important, the next appointment was three weeks from Wednesday—at 5:30 in the morning.

The sort of environment I just described is obviously an *opaque company*. If you expect people to feel trusted, you need to achieve what we think of as a *transparent company*.

In our own case, we strive for transparency in both a literal and figurative sense. One of the most important ways that we are transparent is that we share our sales results with all of our associates. Everyone who works with us can go to any one of our computers and call up the numbers and see how we're doing. That goes for good times and bad times, and thank goodness it's usually been good times. And we're not talking about just quarterly and yearly sales. We share sales figures by the hour, by the day, by the month, by the quarter, by the year, by department, compared to last year, and compared to plan. What's more, we usually conduct a meeting on a quarterly basis of all store employees at which we show and explain these numbers in summary form.

Do banks do that? Hotels? Airlines? Catfish farms?

Well, they ought to.

Since we view our people as our treasured assets, why shouldn't they all know how the business is performing? I mean, they're doing the work, and thus they have every right to see how things are going, and it's an important signal of how much we trust them. Can you imagine if you had a football field without any markings on it and the players weren't allowed to know when they had made a first down and so the game just went on without reason? Or if changes in stock prices were secret, so after you bought a stock you couldn't find out if it was going up or down?

So open things up a little—with certain limits. We're private, and therefore we don't share the bottom-line figures, except with the owners, advisory board, and our bank. The reason is there are too many short- and long-term considerations that affect a host of adjustments that determine those numbers, and so we feel they would be more confusing than illuminating.

The only thing we stress repeatedly is that we do not want our associates sharing the names of our customers who buy this or buy that—invest in a diamond or an expensive suit or whatever. This is our commitment to the personal and private relationship we have with each and every customer.

For us, this transparency creates a bond. Associate after associate who joins our team comments that at first they were amazed and then they appreciated the openness of our sharing our results with them. They immediately feel like a part of the team and they celebrate along with us when we hit the numbers. Or they go the extra mile—"one for good measure," as Mom used to say with a sense of urgency—when we're behind.

It goes without saying that we also have an open-door policy. People can and do see me and Bill and Bob and Russ and the other members of the family all the time and any time. We are on the floor or in our offices; we're visible and available. And we are always ripe and ready to reconnect.

When we renovated our lower-level offices in Westport a few years ago, Russ continued the spirit of transparency by designing most of the office walls using clear glass. People can see that we are working, and when there is a real challenge or the need to talk, anyone can wave to see if they can come in, which of course happens often, and we love it.

I've always liked a phrase coined by Tom Peters a million years ago: "managing by walking around." I especially like "leadership by walking around," because effective leaders know the power of the human connection! It's clear to me that people are more comfortable approaching and talking openly when they're on their own turf, and so leaders need to engage associates in their own territory.

I don't know how good a leader I am, but I do know I walk around a lot, wearing out a considerable amount of shoe leather. I was told that someone has a spoof video on how I make my rounds. And I still do them. I visit every corner of the store, especially after being away for a while, to say hi and shake people's hands and stop occasionally to chitchat or schmooze, which gives everyone an opportunity to engage one-on-one and raise any pressing issue.

When it comes to walking around, no one does it better than Captain Denny Flanagan, a senior pilot extraordinaire at United Airlines who you wouldn't necessarily expect to be walking around. He makes a point during pre-flight meetings with his flight attendants and crew to not only review safety issues but also ways that they can hug their customers and each other. He urges everyone to know people's names. He calls parents to assure them that their children will be well cared for. During a flight, he comes out of the cockpit to greet everyone. He hands out his business card with his phone and e-mail address, and encourages people to call or write him. For associates, he even started a vacation day fund so people can donate their vacation days to colleagues who need an extra day to be with ill spouses or family members. He is remarkable. I've been on board and heard attendants say they request his flights because everyone is so happy flying with him. He says it comes from his heart. He is a genuine hugging captain. It can be done and Denny is living proof.

Another example of our transparency is that I keep an electronic calendar of my whereabouts, and it's open to anyone who wants to see it. And I mean anyone! Clearly, if I have something private, I just mark it private—and I can't remember the last time I identified something that way.

When I'm away, I also always personalize my voice-mail message, saying something like, "Hi, I'm in Italy on a trip with the buying team buying lots of fun and fashionable merchandise for our clients, and I don't have access to voice mail or e-mail regularly. I'll be back March 15. Hope you have a fabulous day!" Anything other than the unforthcoming and uninformative "out of the office." The more transparent you are about your time and what you are doing, the more credibility you have, and that reflects well on your integrity.

We feel strongly that all companies ought to have their team members be able to view the calendars of their leaders. How can you schedule a meeting, or make a meaningful telephone call, if you don't know where the person is and what he or she is doing?

Since we make sure that our customers can call a member of management after hours, we also feel it's only fair that we give out our home phone numbers to our associates, so they can contact owners and managers if something significant comes up after hours. We trust them not to abuse this option, and they don't. I very rarely get calls at home. But when I do, it's urgent and I do my best to respond quickly and appropriately. I know my family and the managers do the same.

Generally speaking, to keep things transparent, it's the responsibility of our team leaders to gather information about the concerns of everyone in their group—Todd Bonner in accounting; Dom, Tullio, Maggie, and Teresa in tailoring; and Andrew and Lauren in advertising and marketing; and so on. And they do it wonderfully.

Occasionally, we have challenges that are interdepartmental, such as a morale issue we experienced in the Richards' tailor shop some time ago. So we set up a committee to discuss things that was spearheaded by Beverly Martin and included Tullio, Pat, and Sylvia. It took time and energy and probing to survey each person involved in the shop. And everyone found the courage to be honest and direct about the goings-on. We took the information and changed some things, and over time the morale improved significantly.

So our preference is to get information directly from our people. It's the way it ought to happen in a transparent, hugging-your-people company.

CHAPTER 13

Build on the Positives and Strengths

You may have heard of the fairly popular management theory of firing 10 percent of your team every year by lopping off the bottom of the totem pole. It sounds awfully harsh, of course, but some business gurus feel strongly that it reenergizes the culture and keeps everyone on their toes. Rather than reenergize a lot of people, I feel it just plain scares the living daylights out of them. It would not only keep me on my toes but wide-awake every night and quaking all day.

If we had adhered to the 10 percent rule when we acquired Marshs, for instance, we would have had to let three or four people go—for no good reason other than to abide by a rigid rule.

Regular reviews on an annual or semiannual basis, though, are terribly important. People want to be advised of how they're doing, and I refer to this approach as building on the positives and strengths.

I will humbly admit that I don't do reviews as well or as often as I should in a formal way. Yet I pride myself that every year since they've joined the business I've reviewed Bob and Russ, my sons and currently our co-presidents. It gets a little tricky all right. And how would you like to be Bob, in charge of all of the men's and women's merchandising and have to review your mother, Linda, who is in charge of women's ready-to-wear and reports to Bob? Interesting, huh? And a few years ago, I insisted that Bob and Russ review me! Thankfully, they concluded that I was pulling my weight and kept me on, because I'm a bit old to work at the car wash or attempt the NFL.

In reviews, I struggle with how to clearly communicate an individual's developmental need or a challenging issue. To me it's a real downer for an associate when you put a negative statement in their review. With some people, when you write down something that's critical of their performance they become very defensive and it often winds up creating even more of a negative.

That being said, it's vital for associates to know where they stand in the eyes of the person they report to (by the way, I don't like the word *boss* because it sounds like you are bossy, and I don't think I'm bossy). So I start with the positives and then weave in constructive recommendations, being very careful about the language I use.

Again, it's emphasizing the positives and the strengths, and if you can look them in their blue or brown eyes and say it— that the future can be brighter than the past—then say it!

As a way of summarizing performance, we don't use a numerical or letter grade system. We feel it's preferable and more mature to go with descriptive evaluations that better communicate someone's range of competency or skill set in various areas.

We do think it helps to isolate areas where a person has to raise the bar. Now, of course, they may not agree and they may come back in your face chapter, text, and verse about why you are wrong, and that's what reviews are all about. They should be interactive exchanges in which you try to discover mutually the value and value added of each associate for the present and the future.

I read about a new personnel policy instituted at a Virginia newspaper where staffers were to be rated on a scale of 1 to 5, but because circulation had been dropping precipitously, everyone was going to be considered a 2, or below average, until things improved. This makes no sense. You can't indulge in blanket assessments, which accomplish nothing other than to make everyone utterly miserable.

The concept of positiveness and building on strengths, which I've done intuitively for years, is reinforced by research undertaken by the Gallup Organization and detailed in the book *StrengthFinders 2.0* (Gallup Press, 2006).

When we do our reviews, we always ask our associates to first do a self-review. And we write our portion of the review before we look at the self-review. It's important that the reviewer must be invested in doing the review and really analyzing the person. He should be like the good student who actually goes to class, listens, and takes notes, and when test time arrives has no need to cram. He only has to glance at his notes and organize his thoughts.

When both the review and self-review are complete, we discuss them. Then the manager consolidates what has been agreed on for the measurable goals for the current year and beyond. In the preponderance of cases, the self-reviews and reviews are very much in harmony. That's a promising sign. It means that there's been enlightening feedback and honest communication, so people really know where they stand.

Sometimes the reviews are one-on-one, and other times I may sit in with the team leader and associate. A year or two ago, Joe Cox, one of the men's team leaders, strongly suggested that I play the role of "Mr. Positive," which of course was easy enough for me. Joe's point was that even if I mention that they need to do more of this or more of that, it pulled them down. So Joe wanted to deliver the constructive criticism and developmental needs part. It worked beautifully and was very well received. I remember vividly doing a review with Joe Biondi, and I'm told that as he left his head was swimming upstream because of the positiveness of our remarks. Later he shared with me and others that it was his most uplifting experience.

He was really motivated and had renewed determination and self-confidence in the areas he is super in. The next year when we sat down at his review, we celebrated that his sales had increased more than 20 percent!

The best way to review people is to go beyond the annual written evaluation and constantly give feedback on how they are doing. That way there are no surprises when the evaluation comes up. It's little understood, but the fact is that hardworking, ambitious associates want clarity and honest discussion of their performance and outlook. They relish a frank appraisal of what they do and have done. That's why many of our associates actually tell us they prefer quarterly performance reviews, especially if they have moved into a new role or position and have assumed different responsibilities.

Here's a good example. Although culturally they were terrific fits, Lisa Coppotelli started on the selling floor and Beverly Martin started in the buying office, and both of them didn't have the skill set or personality required for those jobs and therefore were complete disasters. Wow, what a mistake we made—two great misplaced people! Thank goodness we recognized that culturally they were ideal for us, and so we worked with them and once they were moved into other areas they both became superstars and have built wonderful careers with us.

I've always liked how Jim Collins, who has done such wonderful research on corporations, describes in his book *Good to Great* how associates are riding on a bus and leaders need to ask not only if they have the right players but if they are in the correct seats on the bus. We had to move Lisa and Bev to other seats on the bus, and now they are both thriving and love the new view. We love having them on the Mitchells/Richards/Marshs business bus!

TRY THE FEEDBACK PROCESS

Unfortunately, a lot of reprimanding—I call it negative energy—goes on in the business world. Well, we believe reprimanding is just a big put-down. We prefer to accentuate the positive. When there's a touchy issue, we like to use what we call the feedback process. Whenever we say "feedback," it's our code word for "Can I give you some constructive criticism without your taking it personally?" Or you might say, "Can you separate yourself from your current poor performance? We know you have it in you to do so much better."

Therefore, when you want to point out something an associate is doing wrong—and it could be a dash sensitive or maybe it's a really heavy matter—you say, "Sam, may I give you some feedback?" Most of the time, if the person has been properly educated about the feedback process, he understands it's a nonthreatening method to share. It's not a put-down, it's a genuine way to suggest an alternative.

It could be as simple as, "Sam, may I give you some feedback?"

Sam says, "Yes, of course."

And you say, "Sam, you are a valuable part of our team and I admire you and your contributions so much, but when I'm close to you I can't focus on your pearls of wisdom because your bad breath is distracting me."

When I see anyone reprimanding another person on our team, I get very angry, especially if it's in front of a customer or another associate. And then I take a big deep breath and I let it go. Very soon afterward, I meet privately with the reprimander and give him or her feedback on how they could have handled the situation in a more positive vein.

A hug-your-huggers culture involves praise and not put-downs. Let's face it, our culture prefers a Joe Torre, who was so outstanding as manager of the New York Yankees, who uses praise to improve his players' strengths (and, wow, they grow enormously!) to a Bobby Knight, the Texas Tech basketball coach, who is—at least in my opinion—a yeller and a screamer, and many times puts down his players as a coaching technique. Now, there is no question that both are winners. I know I just couldn't play for Bobby. I believe the people on the Mitchells/Richards/Marshs team wouldn't like it either. We'd all play for Joe in a snap.

We once had a sales team leader who turned out to be a serial reprimander. When this was brought to the attention of her manager, Todd Mitchell, he spoke to her about dealing with issues in a positive light rather than by reprimanding. She just couldn't do it. She was a rules and regulation person through and through. In her eyes, people "shouldn't get away with doing this and doing that," and she wasn't even willing to try Todd's suggestions. Instead, she just quit. She was a Bobby, not a Joe. She simply didn't want to take the time or energy to work things out in a manner that was acceptable to everyone without putting someone down.

Of course, we think it is entirely appropriate to document in personnel files when there has been a violation of company policies or principles. For example, arguing, swearing, or any sort of inappropriate behavior with another associate or customer. We also stick notes in files all the time to record positive deeds and exceptional behavior. And that's what we mostly have—files filled with positive declarations and letters about our great huggers.

One Saturday, Bill was waving a letter around at the morning meeting from a customer praising the sales associates, customer service, and the tailor shop for a fine job they had all done. Well, Elli, who has worked in the tailor shop forever, was at the meeting, and it felt pretty good to hear the praise. A lightbulb went off for her and she came into Pam's office and asked Pam to help her type a letter to the Jewish Home, where her mother lived. So she could "pass it along" and pause to praise the people there who were taking such good care of her mother. And she did. And she felt wonderful about it—especially knowing that Andrew Banoff, the CEO of the Jewish Home, was the type of person to show the letter around and congratulate his staff for a job well done!

Bill and I and the family tell these stories all the time—almost every week. A hugging culture creates an environment where people are comfortable giving and receiving compliments for their contributions—their hugs.

This may not sound like a big deal, but we've had associates who have joined our team tell us that because they have never, ever been complimented by a boss, they never felt comfortable enough to compliment someone they worked with. How sad.

It's fun to see people smile when you pay them a compliment, and it's wonderful to hear them compliment their colleagues in the lunchroom.

Try it today.

Hug someone in a positive way, focusing on their *strengths*!

CHAPTER 14

Check In, Don't Check Up

Doesn't it make you nauseated when you call up a business and before you even reach a live person—and you've plowed through eight mystifying menus—you get these shrill recordings that say, "To better serve you and to help us with customer service, we're going to record this conversation!" And you know darn well that it's to check up on you and the operators. They might as well just blurt out, "We don't trust our people and we don't trust you, so we have to record this conversation to see that everyone behaves!"

Technology has radically changed the workplace, in both good and bad ways. The bad part is that a lot of people feel Big Brother is always watching. They know their phone calls can be monitored, that security cameras can record them, that their e-mails can be read by supervisors. Some companies even equip their associates with geotracking cell phones so bosses know where people are at all times—are they working on that corporate strategy paper or buying a parakeet at the pet store? None of this makes people feel trusted.

But it's more than just technology. It's the managers who constantly come around, call, e-mail—use whatever means available—to see if you're doing your job. They'll ask you ten or twenty times a day: "Did you make that sale?" "Did you finish that report?" "Did you place that call?" Did you, did you, did you?

Here's a story I heard from someone in the computer software world. Jordan was a software salesman, and a top-notch one. He hit his numbers, and usually exceeded them. Yet he had a boss who was an overbearing micromanager. He always wanted to know what Jordan was doing and how he was doing. When Jordan was in the office, his boss would drop by his cubicle a dozen times a day to inquire about accounts. Jordan began to keep a log in his drawer of these visits. One record-breaking day his boss appeared thirty-seven times. On the road, he'd get phone calls, voice mails, e-mails—where was he, how were things going? One time he stopped for gas and while he was filling up the tank, he got a text message alert: "You finish the Appleby visit yet?" He ducked into the bathroom for a moment. Before Jordan could wash his hands, another text message arrived: "Haven't heard back from you on the Appleby account."

This, of course, was extreme. But tamer versions go on all the time. And when they do, associates feel as if they are constantly being checked up on, and that's not a good feeling, nor does it instill trust.

We very much detest the notion of checking up. Naturally

we keep on top of things. What we try to do, however, is *check in*, a much friendlier, more trustworthy, and far less intrusive means of staying in the loop.

Checking in, we feel, is absolutely necessary. Remember, delegation is not abdication. If you don't check in with people, you might as well check out! And if you do that your business is sure to wind up being checkmated!

There's an important distinction between checking in and checking up. Checking in involves restraint and a positive attitude that comes draped in the trust instilled within a personal relationship. If you go to someone as a mentor or coach to assist and suggest, rather than to beat up and demand, you earn respect and trust, and you end up motivating them.

I think Bob Mitchell, one of our copresidents, does a terrific job of checking in on the buying side. He'll say, "How's it going, Dan, on that collection from Loro Piana?" Or "Ellen, wow, it's great to see those new Manolo Blahnik and Prada shoes flying out the door. What are the demographics of the customers buying them?" Or "Dad, have you talked to the team leaders about the new custom-made-to-measure program? What did they think?"

Bob does it in a direct yet soft and probing way, with open-ended questions that allow the associate to respond in an equally genuine open and direct way.

If you have a strong personal and professional relationship, you can then check in with an associate and say, "How are you doing on that contract?" or "How are you doing on the sales forecast for June?" That way, the question should be viewed as a positive by both parties.

If you barge into someone's office and bark, "Haven't you gotten that benefits report done yet?" or "When are you going to make that sales call, already?"—well, that's not checking in. You might as well handcuff the person to a chair and shine floodlights on him.

When someone says, "Hey, I feel like you are checking up on me," you need a means of communication to give feedback to prevent that feeling from continuing. A good way to accomplish this is to suggest a proactive strategy—like arranging to meet once a week with someone to go over loose ends, or to recommend that people copy you on an e-mail when they send it out. It's setting a standard that you want to have positive and anticipated communication.

To come across as checking in rather than checking up, you can say something like, "How's it going?" or "What's happening?" If you have a trusting relationship, they will tell you.

REMEMBER, NO SPYING

We recognize that technology makes things awfully tricky. Candidly, I look at sales reports every day. It's part of my get-up-in-the-morning-and-get-going routine. I look at sales associate numbers for the day and client sales for the day. In the morning, out pops an automatic report that shows every sale over $2,000 from the previous day. What do I get out of this routine? The whole process of getting this data helps to create a sense of urgency, which is essential to driving sales. In addition, 90 percent of the time the results enable me to quickly congratulate and celebrate a great sale with the appropriate sales associate and team leader, and the other times they reveal a need to do some coaching.

Of course, I'm totally aboveboard and very transparent with this, and the sales associates know I'm "looking" at their sales. But I think most of them realize that I am doing this to applaud their work or to coach them and not to check up on them. I'm checking in!

When it comes to checking up on associates using technology, well, that belongs in a totalitarian culture and not a free and open culture where you trust your associates to act responsibly. Regularly looking at someone's e-mail or listening to their voice-mail messages is not for us, that's for sure.

Our philosophy is that we do have the right and are entitled to look at any e-mail that goes over our system, but it would take exceptional circumstances for us to ever do that—like suspicion of illegal behavior. Just like we have cameras that are strategically set up throughout the store; clearly, their purpose is not to check up but to deter and catch shoplifters.

Years ago, for education purposes, I wanted to record how a great seller interacted with a customer using overhead cameras and then having other sellers watch it. And I was shot down immediately by everyone in the room, because they protested that it would feel too much like Big Brother. I hadn't thought about it that way but after our discussion I totally agreed.

The use of mystery shoppers has become very popular at stores, restaurants, hotels, and movie theaters. These are undercover professionals hired by management to pose as real shoppers to check up on customer service. For me, they would feel like spies. So we don't use them. We think that they're one more sign of a lack of trust in your people. I'd rather hear feedback directly from our associates and customers! And vendors! We get input in person or through personalized customer surveys that ask how people feel about the associates who assist them.

Many companies require a doctor's note if someone is out sick for more than a day, or some such schoolmarmish rule. Again, that doesn't sit well with us. We do have a procedure set up where we can ask for a doctor's note, but it rarely happens. I know we did ask one individual, because he claimed he couldn't do some of his work due to his condition. And yet from our perspective he seemed fine. Therefore, we wanted to make sure we had a professional doctor's opinion. He provided it and we respected it.

But as a routine matter, why treat people like kids? If someone says he or she is sick, that's good enough. End of story.

Naturally people take leaves of absences, due to personal matters such as a separation, divorce, or serious illness, including substance abuse. Of course, it's really nice when good things happen to great people, like having a baby or getting married or some other happy and joyful event. When the leave results from illness, we ask for some type of medical documentation. This falls to our human resources people, who we have confidence in to do the right and legal thing. It's a very delicate area these days owing to all the discrimination laws, and thus we make sure to get HR involved so we don't break any laws by trying to be nice guys.

Again, we're checking in, not checking up.

CHAPTER 15

Conflict Resolution: When Winnie Stops Talking to Kristin

It became one of those notorious stories that we chuckle over now but that wasn't so funny at the time. Two of our great sales associates had been getting on each other's nerves. It apparently began innocently enough when they both tried to claim the same customer, as happens from time to time. The ill feelings, however, wouldn't subside and actually worsened. It finally reached the unimaginable point where one accused the other of trying to run him down with his car in our parking lot. Like many conflicts, this one got blown way, way out of proportion, and it did take a lot of investigation to determine whether the incident was purely accidental or premeditated. Clearly, this whole dust-up was not healthy for the team spirit, and an alleged attempted vehicular homicide sure wasn't a hug between the two individuals.

Finally, after several meetings with Bob Mitchell, everyone

agreed that it was accidental, and the underlying squabble was thoroughly resolved and life went on. The associates actually laugh about it now. They demonstrated that they needed help to resolve a big issue between themselves, and they accepted it. Now they get along just fine.

Human nature is human nature, and even in a well-oiled hugging culture like ours conflicts occur. People fight over perceived slights. They get agitated over irritating habits. Kristin, perhaps, was snapping her gum too loudly, and it drove Winnie up the wall. Once I read about two workers who were cleaning the hippo pond at an amusement park and started arguing over cheating at cards, and one doused the other with gasoline and threatened him with a shovel. I've also heard about a drugstore worker who stabbed a coworker during an argument over who could microwave her soup first. Yes, a lot of workplace quarrels arise over silly things like these, some of the same idiocies that families fight over.

It's important not to let bickering and pouting continue. Spats, big or small, sap the team spirit and can irrevocably damage careers—and, as you can see, cause actual terrible injuries. So you can't have people not talking to or snubbing other people. It's awful for team morale. It's especially bad for business if harsh words are exchanged on the selling floor in front of customers. I can recall some rare occasions years ago when—can you believe it?—we had a seller berate buyers in front of customers and other associates over picking out ties: "Why'd you choose these ugly pink ties, they're awful. I can't sell them!" We made it abundantly clear that this behavior was unacceptable and it stopped.

Nevertheless, let's face it, many managers ignore squabbles—which is the worst thing to do—because they're just not comfortable dealing with conflict. I can understand that. For years, I was called a classic conflict avoider over minor issues. I had to learn that often these minor disagreements quickly mushroom into "thermal nuclear war." Squabbles won't mend on their own. In fact, if you don't confront them head-on, they worsen.

In a hugging culture, because there is mutual respect and trust, conflicts get more quickly identified and more effectively resolved. Many organizations have no system to bring conflicts to the attention of someone who can facilitate their resolution. In a hugging culture, because people are open and speak up and there is checking in, quarreling associates have the opportunity to talk about their problems openly rather than letting them simmer. And I like to practice a defined plan to bring them to a resolution.

I call it the Timeout Process.

It's quite simple. As Bob did, the appropriate manager brings the bickering parties into a room and says to them, "Guys, T for timeout—stop the conflict, stop the game, break for a commercial, so things can be aired. Let's talk, let's communicate."

My principal means of addressing conflicts stems from the skills I learned in the book *Parent Effectiveness Training (P.E.T.): The Proven Program for Raising Responsible Children*, which helped me extensively in raising my sons, and I still believe in it. And so when the timeout is called, I follow P.E.T.'s guidance and begin by sharing with the combatants—and I know it may sound silly to some—the fact that there is a conflict, because often one or more people can't even see it. Then the two parties must:

1. Define the conflict clearly—and it's often best to have them write it down. And then you ask the question, "Who owns the problem?" Because if no one accepts responsibility, then it's not going to be resolved. Most of the time, both individuals own pieces of the problem, though sometimes only one does. It doesn't matter. What matters is that they agree on ownership.

2. Show a genuine desire to resolve the issue—this is especially important if the individuals have already tried unsuccessfully to settle things and the conflict has only intensified. You have to look them in their eyes and observe their body language to see if they're sincere. Take the time to let them know that you care and that there is going to be a resolution that will be a win-win-win.

3. Brainstorm ideas that lead toward resolution—and really no ideas are bad ones if they might cool off matters. Often, to get them thinking, we ask things like "How do you perceive yourself? How do you think others perceive you? How do you think Joe [or whoever it is on the other side of the conflict] perceives you?" Then we ask the battlers some nonobvious questions to help them better understand each other, the same sort of questions we might ask during an interview or a reconnect.

When I coach two conflicting parties to a resolution, we sit down together and I often draw a few questions out of my bag of tricks to lighten the mood and hopefully to enlighten everyone about each other. And it makes the personal human connection positive. For example: 1.What are you most proud of? 2. What decade did you have the most fun in? 3. What are your greatest strengths?

Many times I start and respond to my own question to give them an example—for instance, "What I'm most proud of is that I've been married for forty-six years to the same wonderful woman."

I find their answers help us see one another in more human terms. I'll also urge the parties to do proactive hugs. Buy a card for the other person and write a thoughtful message in it. Offer to treat the person to coffee or a beer.

4. Agree to a plan that both believe is a win-win-win resolution—be specific and write it down. It should generally include ways to measure the effectiveness of the outcome, and it should stipulate who is responsible and accountable for which part of the planned agreement. Ask them to check in with each other frequently to ensure that things are still going smoothly.

5. Agree to have a time in the future when you can check in with both parties together—give it a week or two weeks, but don't start the process and then renounce your responsibility to ensure that it's working. You must monitor and facilitate the situation and conduct follow-up sessions as needed, until the air is cleared and a positive working relationship evolves.

Can you resolve every conflict? No. But by using this method, I feel you can resolve more than 90 percent of them, and all those where the parties *truly* want to resolve them. There will always be a few occasions when one person is unwilling or unable to lay down arms—he just can't stomach this other person—despite the Timeout Process and all the well-intended advice we coaches offer. Then I'm afraid it's time to trade the person or persons to another team.

By the way, our two associates who had the parking lot run-in continue to check in with each other almost daily, and they're having fun doing it.

CHAPTER 16

Going to the Moon

One unique way that I help associates through difficult times, give them perspective, and truly deepen my relationship with them is by sitting down with them and "Going to the Moon." It's a special technique that I learned in a former life, and it can be done only when there's a lot of mutual trust.

Moon trips began for me forty years ago, just about when Neil Armstrong so memorably traveled to the real moon. Before joining the family business, I was working as an administrator and fund-raiser at the New England Institute for Medical Research. One day at a performance review with my boss, I was told to my utter shock that many of the scientists didn't like me.

Naturally, I was devastated. I had thought that everyone liked me. I was raising money for them, I tried to be as nice as I could, I was always upbeat. But my boss explained that often my "boyish enthusiasm" slipped into tenacity and I was overpowering people. As a result, they felt that I was putting them down, and they didn't like it.

I sort of wobbled weak-kneed out of that meeting, my face ashen. Have you ever been there? Seeing that I was in distress, and having confidence that he could help me since he knew how much we trusted each other, an older gentleman and fellow fund-raiser sat me down and asked me to accompany him to the moon.

"Where?" I asked.

"The moon!" he replied.

Going to the Moon is an exercise that involves taking an imaginary voyage to the moon. It enables you to regain your bearings, and it deepens trust among associates with remarkable results.

By the time I returned from my first moon trip, I was my old self again. By that I mean I was confident yet had a new perspective on myself and my life. I was prepared to apply a new focus to resolve my issues with the scientists. When I took that maiden trip, I recognized that I wanted everyone to like me, because I am a pleaser at heart, and that sometimes I needed to behave differently with certain people. I didn't always have to tell everyone what I felt was the best way to do something or to monopolize the conversation. Most of all, the moon trip taught me that you can be proactive and change yourself.

Over the years, I've taken associates to the moon when it was helpful for them because they weren't able to see that they were stumbling at work due to outside challenges in their lives. And I've taken moon trips with associates who were suffering from marital problems, substance abuse problems, or gambling addictions. But I never get into the booze or the marriage—we don't even discuss it—because the point of the exercise is not the particular issue but for them to learn how they can modify their own behavior themselves.

They can change. They can change *only* if they want to— really want to!

One person I took to the moon relatively recently was Helene Cote, our good-natured credit manager. She was walking to the copy machine one day, and, trying to be uplifting with a hug, I called out, "How's the great Helene Cote doing?" I expected her to respond that she was doing fine or even terrific. Instead, she started bawling. Normally, she's never unhappy, but here she was unable to stop crying.

Obviously something was really wrong—and, in fact, I quickly realized that she was still deeply grieving, devastated by the death of her brother at the age of forty-eight, which seemed so terribly unfair to her—and so I said, "How would you like to go to the moon?"

"I thought this was nuts," she later told me. "But your name is on my paycheck, so I said, sure."

Helene quickly confided that the loss of her brother had raised a number of personal issues that she had to come to grips with.

So we began.

I said, "Helene, let's close our eyes and visualize this entire mission to the moon. We drove to the airport and flew directly to Cape Kennedy. We got a good night's sleep. Wow, wasn't that relaxing! And we got up the next morning early, slipped on our spacesuits, and before we knew it, it was blast-off time. Vroom!"

It's important to use a calm tone and slow down your speech. It's a matter of taking the whole trip in slow motion.

As we traveled in our spaceship far above, the people on Earth immediately disappeared. Gradually, the Earth became smaller and smaller and the moon became larger and larger.

The farther into space we got, the more relaxed Helene became. After a good long while, we landed on the moon, flipped the steps down, and walked out onto the surface—no, it wasn't green cheese after all—and looked far away to see Earth. And then I removed a powerful telescope from my backpack and set it up and focused it on Earth. And, lo and behold, we saw Jack and Helene, eyes closed in the office in Westport, Connecticut, U.S.A., Planet Earth.

In our visualization, we observed Helene back in my office in control. She got up and made herself a cup of hot tea and made me a cup of black coffee. And we gave each other a high five and a hug.

She couldn't understand why she felt better, just that she did: "It was like the door opened and it let me back in to where I was before. I had felt like I was shaking inside all the time. I stopped shaking. It was amazing."

From the moon, we talked about how it appeared that Helene was in control again and could change anything and do it in a calm, self-confident manner.

Then it was time to head home, and so I said to Helene, "Let's get in our spaceship and blast off!" We took our time with the return journey. Chatting again slowly. The reentry process was smooth and the landing at Cape Kennedy was perfect.

"Okay," I said to Helene, "let's slowly open our eyes, we're back here in reality land."

And then we talked. Helene shared with me that she had seen and felt herself outside herself and was beginning to gain control of her life again. "I feel we've been sitting here for only a few minutes," she said, "and yet I just glanced at my watch and, wow, two hours have gone by!"

She looked at me and said, "Thanks, Jack! It was an inspiring trip and I feel so much better! It was tremendously liberating. Freeing."

A day or two later, she poked her nose into my office and told me straight away that under the circumstances it was the best thing that could have happened to her. She said that I had helped her help herself return to her jolly "old" self.

And then about a week later, as I entered Richards, I bumped into Dan Cote, her husband, who works in our shipping department. And of course I inquired, "How's Helene today?" He started tearing up, but I sensed that these were tears of appreciation as he said, "She went to the moon again and it was another super trip!"

When we traveled to the moon together, Helene trusted me and I trusted her, and the result was that she was able to muster the courage to help herself so she could get back to her job of helping others.

I don't do moon trips often. People have to be ready and willing. But when I do, I find they have a phenomenal impact.

Two people come to really trust each other and gain fresh perspective on their lives.

And then, of course, they can travel solo on future trips.

Anyone can do it anywhere. You don't need a rocket and you don't actually have to journey 238,000 miles from home. The trip to the moon allows you to see yourself interacting with others from another view. It's an exercise in gaining perspective and seeing how your behavior is affecting yourself and others. Furthermore, it helps you to see how relatively easy it is to modify your attitude and actions if you truly want to change.

So if you see someone struggling and you haven't visited the moon lately, I strongly recommend that you put on your space helmet and moon boots and blast off together!

HUGGING STUDY GUIDE # 2

TRUST

No surprises: It's simple common sense and vital to encourage everyone to be forthright and to always tell the truth, and that way you build trust and eliminate surprises.

Have expectations and standards, not rules: Rules are cold and unbending and often destroy trust. Instead, create a list of the expectations you want associates to fulfill.

Establish a New World nation: Don't have a Third World culture with a dictatorial authority. Have one where people are inspired and motivated and enabled to have freedom with responsibility and where it becomes an "Of course" hugging mentality.

Make your company transparent: Do this in both a literal and figurative sense. Share sales results and other measurable figures and goals with associates, and have open offices and electronic calendars for all to see.

Reviews should accentuate the positives: Avoid associate reviews that dwell on shortcomings and use school-like grades that belittle rather than embolden. Stress the positives and strengths, then recommend ways to improve, grow, and appreciate accomplishments.

Check in: Some companies love to check up endlessly on associates. Forget that and go easy on intrusive technology. Instead, check in—it's a hug, a more positive, softer way of keeping everyone in the loop.

Call timeouts: Conflicts between associates happen even in hugging cultures. Don't ignore them. Call a timeout and gather around the table to smooth out the differences. Come up with a win-win-win plan that everyone can accept and that enhances a positive, personal, and professional relationship.

Go to the moon: To really deepen trust among associates, take them on an imaginary moon trip that will grant them greater control over their lives and watch them change themselves by gaining a new perspective.

PART THREE

Pride

The Power of All of Us

CHAPTER 17

Feeling You Are the Business

Often I'll have just finished a great meal at a restaurant, and I'll want to pay and leave, and yet when I try to locate my waiter it's as if he had entered the Witness Protection Program. I'll try to flag down another waiter or the maître d', and you would think I had become invisible. I'm sure it's happened to you.

Or I'll drop into a deli and the two guys behind the meat counter will be talking about last night's hockey game and not care a whit about taking my order for a half pound of roast beef and a quart of coleslaw. I think of these as "spiritless workers," because they go through the motions without thinking or really caring about their jobs. What it boils down to is they have no pride in what they're doing.

On the other hand, I believe we are "spirit full people"! We hear it all the time from our associates: "We're proud to be working with you." That's because they feel great about the image of our business, and they feel that they are an integral part of the business. And they are proud of it.

They feel they are the store.

Pride follows Nice and Trust because when you work in an open environment where associates have the highest integrity and are very comfortable, then people develop pride. Big-time. And that pride exists on several levels, including the inner self-satisfaction of excellent accomplishments and the outer prestige of family, community, and friends. When we speak of pride, we mean pride in the company, pride in individual performance, and lots more.

Pride is a potent motivator. After all, are you going to work as diligently for a company you're ashamed of? When you feel pride in an organization, you don't tell new people you meet that you're a banker, you say that you're an investment banker at Lehman Brothers or a wealth adviser at Bank of America. You don't say you're a mechanic, but you're a mechanic at Midas. You're not a clothing salesperson, you work at Mitchells/ Richards/Marshs.

In other words, when you like to give the name of the company, that means you're proud of it. You expect people who hear the name to be impressed that you work there. I confess that I haven't worked in another environment in a long time, but I am told that at places where people don't feel this sense of pride there is not nearly as much motivation and commitment. No one seems to want to go the extra mile or even hundred yards, and there's more of a nine-to-five mentality. You notice this when you get to a grocery store at seven p.m. and the associates who can see you through the door wave hello but won't let you in.

Everything stops dead at seven p.m.

Now, naturally, you can go overboard with the pride thing. I don't think you need to have a framed photograph of the chief executive officer hanging over your mantel at home to feel pride. It doesn't mean that if you hear a slur hurled at the company that you challenge the offender to a fistfight.

But pride is an incredibly powerful force for cultivating loyalty. And it has to be fed with good stock all the time. Studies often show that associates feel a lot of pride when they start a new job, but that it steadily erodes with time. That's because companies don't systematically work at maintaining pride—an important factor in motivating associates to stay for life and have a career with you.

So how do you build pride?

Sharon Behrens, director of consumer experience, U.S. Retail, the "Chief Hugger" for Nike, has a wonderfully creative way to instill pride in associates by capitalizing on the company's brand history. She created a Nike "History and Heritage 1957–2006" poster for the staff that gets placed in the store break rooms. When associates have a significant anniversary, she includes that date alongside the other essential names and dates that have made Nike the success it is today. Imagine how proud it must make someone feel to see her name and the anniversary of her hire date on the same poster as the date Michael Jordan signed on to endorse Nike. They frame it and Nike founder Phil Knight signs it as a special keepsake for the associate.

WITH US

A big part of it is making it clear that everyone's job counts—*really* counts—whether they're on the floor or behind the scenes. So you have to demonstrate consistently to everyone that what they do contributes to the well-being of the business. I always try to use the preposition *with* rather than *for* when I speak about our associates. People work *with* us, not *for* us. It's one word but it makes a huge difference in attitude.

In many companies, there is often a tension between the sellers who are the most visible associates and seem to reap most of the glory, and the behind-the-scenes people. We constantly talk about how everybody contributes, *everybody*! It's not just the quarterback and running back but the special teams and the backups who jump in when there are injuries. Everyone helps win the game. We have many rituals that emphasize this, such as regular all-store meetings and the CEO letter I write each week that gets sent to *all users.*

I think it helps that we have several family members who are not directly involved in the front lines of sales: Russ, Andrew, Linda, and Tyler, who balance Bill, Scott, Bob, Chris, Todd, and me in the sales roles. This balance creates a fabulous interdependent feeling from an ownership perspective. And it helps remind us when we go overboard with accolades that focus only on the sellers. What's more, during busy times of the year most of the "nonselling" associates get an opportunity to work on the floor, or to become involved with customers through gift-wrapping, mailings, deliveries, and so forth. Everyone can thus feel ownership.

Not long ago, Eugene, one of our sales associates at Marshs, had a customer who needed a suit for his son's funeral. This was obviously a horrific tragedy, and naturally Eugene got the suit ready for him the same day. When Eugene shared this heartbreaking news with Chris Mitchell, Chris said, Let's send some flowers to the family, which Eugene did. And later the man came in to personally thank Eugene and Marshs for the kind gesture.

And Eugene said to us, "I really felt proud of working at Marshs. Since you guys took over we do a lot more of this than ever before." And Chris chimed in, saying, "You know what, Eugene, next time you don't need to run this by me. Of course, I want to know about the sad and joyous stories, but you can pick up the phone and order flowers as needed."

That made Eugene feel even prouder.

To build pride, we feel you need to start with four essential criteria:

1. An inspiring corporate mission statement: It's important that you have a statement of purpose that conveys strong values and worthy principles so associates feel they are doing good by working with you. We share our mission statement with all of our associates. Mission statements help associates appreciate the ultimate importance of what they do. We like to educate our associates about the value of clothing: when people look good they feel good, and so the associates see how the work they do brings self-confidence and a sense of pride to others.

Associates should also be taught the corporate history, so they know about the founders and their values. Marco Greenberg of Reel Biography created a wonderful tribute film that traces our company history. It focuses on the family and the people that have made our business grow from three suits to too many to count. Many, many associates have commented that they appreciate hearing the stories and seeing the pictures of our humble beginnings, and there's not a dry eye in the house when they view it.

2. A clean and attractive work environment: Nobody feels proud of a shabby workplace—tattered carpeting, water dripping from the ceiling every time it rains, rodents scampering around. Clearly, we have physical environments that we feel are among the best in the world, and we make a point of renovating them on a regular basis—for the benefit of our customers, but just as importantly for the benefit of our associates. Indeed, our associates share with us that they constantly get comments from their friends and customers, such as "Wow, it must be great to work in a store that is as beautiful and comfortable as this one!" And they reply, "It sure is!"

3. Up-to-date, user-friendly technology: It's a huge source of pride when our associates are talking to their family or friends who work elsewhere and are able to say that we are leaders in technology to serve our customers in a personalized way. To be able to point out that we know every single sale to every single customer in Westport since 1989 is nothing but a wow!

In every sense, the technology is extremely user-friendly. I always kid that even grandparents like Linda and me not only were able to learn the systems but now depend on them. Others feel great about being able to work from home using our technology, and some do it on a regular basis. Helene in accounts receivable often works from home, because she is tied in with our computer and telephone lines seamlessly.

A great idea that Todd Mitchell introduced was pagers. For years, we had this loud, obnoxious overhead paging system. It sounded like something from Caldor, the now-defunct discount store: Bill Mitchell's unique voice shouting, "All associates to the front desk! All associates to the front desk! Please, downstairs associates to the customer service desk!" It did work. They came scampering up from downstairs. But we sure weren't proud of it, because it sounded just awful. Today, Bill gets the downstairs crew's attention (Eliza, Betsy, JoAnn, Laurie, Dennis, James, and the rest) by sending very quiet vibrations to their pagers (which reminds them of Bill's fondness for massages), and they look at their beepers and run upstairs to the customer service desk.

It's another hug to our huggers that they can determine whether or not their colleagues are in the store by simply looking at a computer screen. In the old days, you had to go searching around for Frank or Phyllis, not knowing if they were in the dressing room or on vacation in Puerto Vallarta. Now you know with a flick of a finger!

4. Educational opportunities: We've always viewed our hugging culture as a learning environment. We believe strongly in learning for life. Once you stop learning, it's basically all over. So we have a Mitchells Hug University that offers courses to our associates in everything from Hugging 101 to Advanced Placement Hugging. We have a board of education that oversees it and a full-time person, Robert Greenfield, who spearheads it, and we primarily draw upon our own staff to function as professors.

The stated mission of the university is to provide our associates with innovative and fun educational programs that contribute to the development and success of each individual and team, supporting them as they deliver world-class customer service to one another and to clients, customers, and friends.

We make a point of doing cross-training throughout the store, which engenders a sense of teamwork. For instance, almost everyone in any capacity uses the AS400 system and knows how to ring up a sale. Iren from accounts receivable fills in for the receptionist, and Tia, Jean, Vicki, Dotty, and Denise from customer service help marketing with mailers, and of course everyone makes deliveries.

We're also huge advocates of people finishing college and advancing to graduate school while working with us. Over the years many have done so. Our feeling is that the more they learn, the more everyone benefits.

Over and over again, our people say things like Debbie Mazza has said, "I feel like family here!" And she's been here only a year. Domenic Condoleo echoes that sentiment. And he's been here for forty-six years. It's the power of pride!

CHAPTER 18

Throw Your Personal Party at the Office

People often beam with pride about their home, and that's perfectly understandable. It's theirs. It's where they live, and its essence reflects their tastes and values. But you rarely hear anyone boast about their workplace—I mean, who says, "Wait until you see my great office, you're going to love the coral color scheme and the soft lighting"—even though many of them spend more time there than at home.

Well, we want our associates to think of where they work in the same context as where they live. It should be another home, just as important as a weekend house.

For starters, we don't use the word *workplace*. To me, it connotes that it's only a place where you work, and we think of it in a much broader sense. We like to say "store," and if I were in the newspaper business I might say "newsroom." Many restaurants also say "the store." Pilots, I have to believe, say "the airport."

It's a lot softer to use the generic name of where you "work," or, as we like to say, where you have fun doing what you've decided to do for a career.

Not only is it our vision that our store is our home, but the Richards store was actually designed to intentionally look and feel like a spacious home where we welcome guests (customers). We have a living room (shoe department), kitchen (customer service and refreshment bar), bedrooms (dressing rooms), and other classic (Zegna, Ralph Lauren, Canali, Loro Piana) and modern (Dolce & Gabbana, Armani, Gucci, Prada) areas of our home.

Other ways that we try to make work feel like home is that owners, managers, leaders, and entry-level associates are all expected, as they might be at home, to pick up after themselves, offer coffee to guests, open the door, walk the customers to their cars, and share a bite to eat or a soda in the lunchroom together.

One important bit of logistics is that we make it clear that we are all on equal footing in these responsibilities. No one gets any special privileges just because their last name happens to be Mitchell. There is no pecking order, nor any sacrosanct turf—no assigned parking places and no executive dining rooms, just as there aren't at home. People have offices, but they can be used by others when their regular occupants are on vacation or out of town.

Dad always used to say, "I empty the trash and serve the coffee at the store and at home, just like everybody does." It was true for him and is true for Bill and me, and it's true for our sons, and we firmly believe our associates see this and feel it. Bill, in fact, is known as Mr. Clean, because he's always scurrying around picking up after all of us!

Associates are encouraged to feel free to occasionally bring their kids to the store. It's a tradition that Mom and Dad established with our sons and nephews. They all started as ten- or twelve-year olds, and had loads of fun first picking up pins, then serving coffee, and, in the old days, yes, sherry. And now our sons escort their children in during the holiday season, among other times, as do many of our associates. In fact, we don't find any need to have a "Take your child to work day," because everyone already brings their family members to the stores.

A lot of companies get all bent out of shape over nepotism. Well, we're thrilled—indeed, we think we're hugging our huggers when entire families come to work with us. And so Richards store manager Jeff Kozak's two daughters work with us, and John Hickey III (whose dad, John Hickey Jr., by the way, worked at Richards for more than thirty years) has contributed two sons. One day, Sophia brought in her husband, Bob, and before he got away we ended up hiring him full-time as "Bartender/Barista Bob," and now he works in shipping and receiving to boot. Tullio happened to bring his brother Pat into the tailor shop twenty-plus years ago, and, lo and behold, Tullio and Pat now manage the shop. All of Tullio's children—two sons and a daughter—have worked at Richards, as have Angela's daughters and Belinda's son and daughter and Amy's son and, thank God, many, many others!

We hired Allison Borowy's son David to work on Saturdays

and a couple of afternoons each week. "It's been fabulous for me, because it's strengthened our already close relationship," Allison said. "You know how challenging most teenagers are. By working at the same place, David really came to understand and respect what I do and how hard I work. At the same time, all the associates treated him like an equal. Do you know how special it is for a young man to feel like an equal, like he's an adult?"

The broad point is that we have an extended family in every sense. As far as we're concerned, bring in those spouses and kids so we can put them on the payroll!

Yes, it's true that occasionally it doesn't work out, and what generally happens is that both the parent and the child realize that it's not clicking and the next day or season the person quietly finds another job. But most of the time the relatives blossom into great associates.

People feel so much like family, entirely at home in our stores, that Jeff Kozak, who spends far more time at the store than at home, said it just felt right to him that he should have his fiftieth birthday party at his home away from home that he is so proud of. In a real sense, it's the house that Jeff helped build.

He asked if he could, and of course we said yes. So he invited his family and friends, many of whom work or have worked at Richards, including the former owners, Ed Schacter (whom we still call the boss) and his daughter Susan Fleisher. All the Mitchells had the opportunity to toast him and say nice things about Jeff. He was just glowing with pride as he stood on the Stairway to Heaven that leads upstairs, with his family and friends spread out in front of him.

I'm so very proud of Jeff, and proud that we have a store to host the birthday party of a hard-working, loyal associate of twenty-nine years. Wow, who else would throw his birthday party where he works? Would your associates?

Never heard of it before. The great Jeff Kozak did it! Fun time!

CHAPTER 19

Reaching into the Community

No business operates in a cocoon. Surrounding it are scores of other businesses and people and needs, big needs and small ones. I'm talking about the larger community. To feel good about your own business, you need to believe it's a proper corporate citizen. That means you have to reach outside to feel good inside and achieve inner pride.

We believe that it behooves us to be consistently involved in community events and by doing things like taking tables at charity events and collecting holiday gifts for needy kids in the inner city. This is not some small side strategy, but a bone-deep belief situated at the core of our business. It's always been one of our priorities.

I like to say we have three C's: Customers, Community, and Cash.

We support literally hundreds of first-rate organizations,

including Kids in Crisis; the Breast Cancer Alliance; the Jewish Home for the Elderly; the Congregational Church; the Inner City Education Foundation; Interfaith Alliance; hospitals in Greenwich, Norwalk, and Bridgeport; Yale; and Sloan Kettering. A laundry list isn't the point. The point is that the associates can be proud that we contribute to so many excellent charities and that they are able to participate in these efforts. We invite them to attend local YMCAs, cancer walks, the swim across the sound, the adopt a pet event (Andrew seems to acquire a new dog every season).

Bill is the absolute leader in our community charitable efforts. In particular, he's heavily involved with Inner City for Catholic Charities. There is a black-tie event for a charity pretty much every week. Mitchell family members routinely attend. But we're not interested in hogging the glory. Bill and all the rest of us enjoy having our associates in attendance when we receive community recognition, because we want others to know that we believe it's in the power of all of us to have the good hearts and make our stores what they are. When they meet their customers in a charitable social setting, they feel privileged to be a part of giving back to the community. It especially makes them feel good about who they are and who they work with. When they come to these events, you can see them swelling with pride.

When the company gives, associates pick up on it, and they give, too. Lisa Coppotelli and Helene Cote make a point of gathering toys and gifts for poor kids. In fact, they got an award for their efforts, and as they stood up onstage and celebrated with their families and the Mitchells in attendance, everyone felt tremendously proud. Huge hugs!

And our business conviction is, don't just enter the community but invite the community into your business. We regularly use our stores to host charitable events—in fact, I'll bet well over a thousand events have been conducted at them. For the last twelve years, for instance, we've hosted a big benefit at Mitchells—annually raising more than $1 million—for the Near & Far Aid Association that helps inner-city children with education and aid. The place is packed from wall to wall.

In Greenwich, Richards sponsors a huge fashion show benefit for the Breast Cancer Alliance, which helps raise awareness of the disease and funds research. Last year, the event contributed more than $1.4 million to their efforts.

Associates who attend these events at the store leave feeling very proud that they work with a business that supports the community. And they have tons of fun.

Another thing that happens is that many of our great customers come to us—it seems as if it occurs almost every day— and ask if we'd like to give to their favorite cause, and we try our very best to be supportive. Often it's through our associates that these requests come, and by responding in the affirmative we're bolstering their relationship with customers and bolstering their own pride, because they see that we care about the ideas they present to us.

One area we try to be careful about is politics, which can get awfully touchy and emotional. Our policy is not to take a stand on any political issue or support a politician inside the store.

We don't allow tables outside the store, nor do we let politicians meet and greet customers inside or outside the stores.

Members of the family have been active in some shape or form in the political process. It's no big secret that the Mitchells have individually supported candidates, and not always the same ones. But we never frame it as the store backing anyone, because that discourages divergent views among our associates.

On a couple of occasions, members of the family have even served in an elected office. Linda was twice elected to the board of education in Wilton, and Dad served several terms on the board of finance in Westport. They were amazingly good public servants and we were all proud of their contributing to our communities.

Jim Nantz has publicly stated numerous times that he is proud to be friends with the Mitchells team because our stores give back to the community. Even if people don't shop with us, they know us. Because of the reputation we have in Westport and Greenwich, people want to work for us. We've even had associates come to us and say that their own bosses had recommended they join our team, saying, "If you have the opportunity to work with the Mitchells, go for it!"

CHAPTER 20

Spread the Word

When good things happen, don't keep the news quiet. Trumpet it throughout the business. A key role of leadership is to celebrate and share acts and deeds of glory and to spread the hug. I'm not talking about false immodesty, since we're big believers in humility. But as Will Rogers famously said, "If you can do it, it ain't bragging." So if you've done it, let your associates know.

Mom and Dad taught us it's even better to use praise from others about you and your associates and business, rather than bragging about yourself. It makes everyone feel good inside.

Just the way Andrew Mitchell and Lauren Monin and Taffy Parisi feel when our customers and associates praise them and we win awards for the best marketing pieces and advertising. Or when the store is honored by being included in *GQ, Esquire,* or *MR* (*Menswear Retailing*) as among the top ten stores in the country or the world. Or when we're named the top designer jewelry store. Or when Bill gets honored at the Jewish Home for the Elderly or I am chosen by *DNR* (*Daily News Record*) as one of the top retail visionaries in retail in the last fifty years. We are all proud of these things. But we always stress that we are proud because of the extended team that has enabled us or the store to be so honored. Remember, nobody does it alone— it's a team effort.

Stories are very powerful and can bring people together around pride. Often in my CEO letter, I try to include a story that we can all be proud of. Here's an example from a recent issue:

"A Company-Wide Hug!"

Dear all,

Todd Mitchell has shared a company-wide hug with each and every one of you today! Todd told me that he had received a call this week from a good friend who is a partner at Goldman Sachs:

My friend was in an equity meeting with a certain billion-dollar retail clothier, discussing how the company could grow and move toward their next Wall Street offering, said Todd.

The company stated that one of their growth plans was to dramatically increase their level of customer service. My friend asked how they planned to accomplish this. Without hesitation, they stated that they would aspire to reach the caliber of Mitchells, Richards, and Marshs. My friend smiled of course; the billion-dollar company did not know that he was a personal friend of mine! He asked a few more

questions and found out that they plan to give each of
their managers a copy of *Hug Your Customers*. My friend
said that if they could indeed become more like Mitchells,
Richards, Marshs, their next equity offering would be the
easiest job he would have this year!

Of course, no one will ever come close to approaching
the style, class, and sophistication of the original. Hats off
to you all for contributing to our groundbreaking success
in treating each customer as a friend. No one does it better!

We especially make a big point of spreading the word about
deeds of honesty, because we think that our associates are
proud that they work in an honest culture. We have a remarkable record of never having had a customer who has lost his
wallet or her purse in the store who hasn't had it returned.
Many times there are hundreds and even thousands of dollars
in the wallet, and the associate who found it has given it back
with nary a dollar missing.

Not long ago at Richards, for instance, a customer service
associate came across a wallet containing $3,000 and no identi-
fication. She immediately gave it to Scott, and about fifteen
minutes later a customer called and said, "By any chance, did
someone find a wallet in the dressing room?" And of course the
customer service person who answered the phone knew exactly
where it was—up in the safe!

What happens is that men will often try on different trousers
and forget to remove their wallet from one of the pairs, and the
pants somehow get put back into stock. One time many years

ago, we didn't find a missing wallet for six weeks. When it was first reported, we had rooted through every trouser in the man's size. Weeks later, lo and behold, someone was trying on a suit and there it was. We called the owner and he was thrilled.

We're proud of all of this. These episodes remind me of what used to occur in the old days when we were much smaller. When someone would come in and pay by cash, some might assume that I would take half and Bill would get half. And both Bill and I took great pride in going right to the cash register, counting out the cash, and saying, Thank you very much, Eleni or Ferdie, and everyone could see how every dollar went into the cash drawer.

In many environments—Enron is the one we remember best—numerous people saw misdeeds going on, and only one or two blew the whistle. In our hugging culture, the few times we've had an internal theft the leads have come from our associates. When they witness irregular behavior, they talk to one of our managers or security with confidence that they are not going to be punished or shunned, but rather quite the opposite. Once we determine that it's true, they get a slight reward, and if they want to—sometimes they do, sometimes they don't—they get recognition from our team for a job well done.

Shoplifting is also a challenge, and we have a wonderful security team that couldn't exist without the complete cooperation of all our associates. Everyone celebrates when John or Charles or Mike and one or two associates work together to catch professional thieves. Even though it's playing on a negative, it becomes a real positive. We're all proud.

All the time, we try to boost pride by reminding everyone of how rewarding their hard work has been. Just before the holidays, after our first year owning Marshs, Chris Mitchell recited a poem he wrote in front of the Marshs team at a Saturday morning meeting, touching on some of the many exciting events that the team faced together during 2006. Here's an excerpt:

Early mornings, late nights, it was harder than you think,
When we just couldn't take it anymore, we hit JDs for some drinks!

We had dust, we had floods, almost everything you can imagine
Definitely NOT the normal stuff when you think of retail and fashion.

In April we took big strides and changed the way you were paid,
We even opened the floor; I'm glad you all stayed!!

Spirits were high, the teamwork even higher,
We were crushing the plan, we were definitely on fire.

Summer came and summer went, the fall had arrived!!
We could all see the excitement, brewing in our customers' eyes.

The parties were a hit, you could hear the buzz around town
We had the best store, the best clothes, the best TEAM . . . hands down.

So this morning as I stand here, I raise my glass and toast all of you
For making year one so special. Here's to an even better year number 2!!

Several companies I'm familiar with spread the word by reprinting positive articles that quote an associate and send them to clients and customers of those associates. Other corporations create a scrapbook of their exciting business achievements as well as the personal and professional successes of individual associates and make it available in the lobby or break room for all to see, share, cheer, and celebrate.

When there's good news to spread, we naturally expect that everyone will welcome it. That means we want our three stores to be competitive with the world, but not with one another. Once one of our big hitters in Greenwich, who was fiercely competitive, didn't quite get this. During Saturday morning meetings of the women's department, Scott would announce the sales numbers by saying something like, "Westport is up 20 percent and Greenwich is up 15 percent." Everyone would cheer, except this woman, who would remain mute. She would cheer only when Greenwich had beaten Westport.

And so in a nice, polite way, we advised her that that sort of favoritism was not part of our culture and that we had to cheer Westport on just as they had been supportive when we started the Greenwich business. We told her that we understood her competitiveness, but that we are really one store with multiple locations.

She got it! One store, three locations. She sees now that pride is bigger than geography.

CHAPTER 21

The Sound of Two Hands Clapping

Who doesn't like a terrific party? I sure do.

Celebrating is a terrific way to build pride, and so we do a lot of it. It doesn't take much at all to get us to break out the bubbly and cheese. We do it as an explicit acknowledgment of some-one's contributions (an anniversary party at Richards), out of happiness for a personal milestone (someone getting married), for a worthy side effort (the accomplishment of writing a book), or to applaud a private interest (an important cause). It's practi-cally gotten to the point where someone can come in with a new hairdo and we're ready to throw a party.

We routinely give our huggers birthday cakes on their birth-days, and often right out on the selling floor. One company I've visited, AlphaGraphics, does something that we're now trying to copy: They ask their associates, Do you like chocolate cake or vanilla cake, or do you even like cake at all? That way, the birthday celebrant doesn't just get a cake, but the flavor of cake that he or she loves—or a fruit platter for that matter! And if you don't like cake or fruit but love mozzarella sticks, well, you get mozzarella sticks.

We don't necessarily bother with bakeries for our sweets. We don't need to. Martha, an associate at Mitchells, on special request from her fellow associates who know her sterling talents in the kitchen, often makes most of the birthday goodies. We call her the Martha Stewart of Mitchells!

These little celebrations quickly become joyous. One busy Saturday at Richards we had one, and the customers themselves really got into it, singing and celebrating right along with the associates. "Feels just great!" said one of Naki's best customers. I don't think you'd see this at a lot of other companies, but you ought to!

We've loved hosting bridal and baby showers since way back in Mom's era. It's a tradition that goes back almost fifty years. For instance, Alethea Gordon, a young lady in customer service sales support, was recently engaged to be married and somebody asked whether we could do an all-store surprise shower. Of course we could. A wonderful surprise party was organized directly after work. About seventy-five associates stayed to celebrate her happiness, and it blew Alethea away.

A&K Railroad Materials includes a calendar in its monthly newsletter noting significant events, and among those significant events are the birthdays of any associates. Josh Ginsberg, a young man from another company whom I met on a trip, told me that in his office they send e-mails to everyone in the office announcing, "It's Bob's birthday."

So we've begun doing these things. The other day, I e-mailed the family that it was Bob Castonguay's birthday (we know him as Bob the Builder, since he handles all of our construction needs), and when I bumped into Bob he said with a huge smile on his face, "What's this about everyone in your family wishing me happy birthday?"

Large celebrations are one of our specialties. Not long ago, we had a big bash to celebrate our ten-year merger of Richards with Mitchells. There were a lot of people from all three stores and it was an upbeat experience for everyone. It made people proud.

We always throw huge holiday parties at our stores: Chris is renowned for playing the keyboard, Scott gets on the guitar and—would you believe it—our head of security, Mike Barrett, plays the saxophone! Yes, even our head of security is a hugger. We sing and eat and dance the night away together just like families do. No one would think of leaving before hearing Scott and Sophia teasing everyone in their annual poem!

In-store fashion trend meetings are highlighted by the latest homemade goodies that Linda and Bob prepare for the fifty-plus associates that attend each season. And the one season that they couldn't cook because they were so busy buying new fashion collections in New York and Europe, it was like, Wow, you forgot the turkey at Thanksgiving.

We also have a big summer picnic that we hold at Compo

Beach in Westport. All of the associates from the three stores are invited, as are their families and significant others. It's a great opportunity for everyone to bond and have a good time and feel proud. I heard one of our associates say, "I'm so happy to share with my family how proud I am of where I work." Four or five years ago, the third-generation Mitchells (we call them the 3Gs) decided it would be fun if they did the cooking and serving, with some help from their kids, the 4Gs, plus a few Mitchell regulars like Lisa Coppotelli and Helene Cote. The 2Gs (Bill and Sue, Jack and Linda) occupied themselves by schmoozing with everyone else. This really set the stage and spirit of the entire evening. Besides good food, we'll usually have games and give away shirts and tote bags.

We try to have all-store meetings quarterly or at least biannually, and we celebrate achievements both in sales and tenure of associates, as well as anything else that we can be proud of. We're so hooked on celebrating, in fact, that any time we have any sort of meeting we try to celebrate something. It could be the great sales from the day before. Or, if we have had a terrible day, we emphasize the positive—for example, the year-to-date sales—or dwell on a special hugging story. If we have to, we'll celebrate the nice weather that day.

Some people don't like to have the spotlight trained on them, like Domenic Condoleo. We honor that, but when a true milestone is reached, we try to figure out some way to slip in an appropriate celebration. Dom recently celebrated his forty-fifth anniversary with us. Because he's uncomfortable with attention, Bill and I had to fake him out by saying we were going to take him to dinner to celebrate, which we did of course, only there were fifty additional people at the dinner! They all toasted and roasted the great Domenic Condoleo.

STAND UP AND CLAP

An important point is that we always try to clap when we celebrate. (When I was at Wesleyan, rather than clapping to acknowledge someone, I would snap my fingers, and I still do this at times. It's another easy way to make some noise, and now some of our associates snap because they've seen me doing it.) The clapping started years ago after I gave Belinda a Ken Blanchard book in which he mentioned the power of clapping. All of a sudden, Belinda started clapping every time someone was praised for a meaningful accomplishment. Over time, it has really caught on. There is something magical about clapping, and when it is an extra-special celebration we try to stand up and clap, delivering a standing ovation.

After all, how often have you received a standing ovation? I imagine never. You've probably participated in a few—at the ballpark when a player swatted a walk-off home run or at the hockey game when the winning goal slammed into the net in triple overtime. And you joined in because you felt great about what you had just witnessed. But can you imagine what it feels like to be on the receiving end?

Why don't more places give a tribute and offer a standing ovation while the person is still working at the company, rather than on their last day before retirement when one foot is already out the door? There are usually gifts and some halfway decent champagne and a string of heartfelt tributes. Finally, there will be a standing ovation, but probably simply because everyone is already standing when the ceremony takes place. But the reason I find these events strange is that at many companies this is the only time an associate is treated so warmly.

There's nothing wrong with these rituals—we do them, too. Vicki, a tailor who had worked with us in Westport for almost thirty years, recently retired, and the Mitchells had a special, meaningful dinner with everyone in the tailor shop. At the end, I asked everyone to get up and give her a standing ovation, which brought tears of joy to her eyes. Everyone in the restaurant could feel the power of that ovation.

A year or two ago, Scott Mitchell had a creative idea at a customer service dinner where he literally went around the room and told a thirty-second story about how each customer service associate was special. Everyone clapped and celebrated, and boy did those associates have great big smiles!

Scott did another fun thing when we were proud to have Michael Kors, one of America's leading designers, make a personal appearance and bring his fashion show to Greenwich. Scott stood on the runway before the show began and said something like, "Great designers don't normally speak, they let their clothes do the talking. But I think if we clap a little, or even a lot, then we might be able to get Michael to come out and say a few personal words to all of you." Of course Michael did, and he said some very nice things about our customers and associates. I could sense how proud all of us were that night.

You might even consider trying preliminary standing ovations. At conferences of Crown Council, an organization of dental practices, the audience is always asked to give speakers a standing ovation when they're introduced, *before* they've even uttered a word. It warms them up and also prepares the audience to listen. I can tell you it worked for me when I was a speaker. I was so warmed up I almost had to take my jacket off. And, believe me, it's sure nice to get another standing ovation after the speech, too.

Not only does a standing ovation make the recipient immensely proud, but everyone else in the organization as well. So we're big advocates of standing ovations. I heartily applaud them.

HUGGING STUDY GUIDE #3

PRIDE

Make people feel they are the business: Have a solid, yet simple, inspiring mission statement that states how important people are, create an attractive work environment with up-to-date and highly accessible technology, and offer continuous educational opportunities.

Make the workplace an extension of home: Design your workplace to feel as warm and inviting as a home, and encourage people to bring in their kids and even hold parties at the office.

Embrace the community: You need to contribute to causes in your community, and make associates part of it, and it's even better if you bring the events into your workplace. Focus on charities and programs that parallel your company's guiding principles. Steer clear, though, of politics.

Spread the word: When good things happen to the business, make sure everyone knows about them; share pearls of praise from other folks in person, in meetings, on the bulletin board, in company written communications—and a poem doesn't hurt.

Cheer them on: It's a big deal—really big—to celebrate accomplishments of the business and the people and to do this consistently, and there's no better way than with standing ovations.

PART FOUR

Include

The Five I's

CHAPTER 22

You Can't Do It Alone

How often do you hear that familiar cry among employees: "No one ever talks to me around here?" You know what they're really saying—that the company doesn't care about their opinions. They never ask them: "What do you think?" Not even about the lunch menu.

Everyone knows how it feels when you have good ideas that will make a project just sing, but the boss says or the rules say that you can't become involved. You would just respond, "The heck with it, I'll just go home at six o'clock." Or maybe out of frustration leave at five. Motivation declines and you create mediocrity rather than excellence. Ultimately, you find that your best people, the great players, will leave to find a company where they can be included.

Once you're Nice to your team and you Trust them and instill them with Pride, you've made a big difference in what sort of culture you have created. But you have to do more! You're not all the way there. You have to also *Include* everyone, which sounds simple but often isn't.

I'm talking about a concept that goes beyond teamwork and feeling part of a process to a deeply rooted sensibility that everyone has that they are an intrinsic and irreplaceable part of the business, that their views and their actions not only count but are crucial and therefore regularly solicited. In short, everyone's in the loop. It's a matter of cleansing the culture of the "we versus they" mentality that persists between the rank-and-file and management in so many companies. The "we" come up with the ideas and the "they" carry them out, like it or not.

This reminds me of when a competitor of ours changed its compensation plan a few years ago. It came exclusively from the top and was essentially presented to associates on a take it or leave it basis. Nobody asked the sellers ahead of time what they wanted—and what they preferred was much different from what management preferred—but rather they were just told what the changes were!

We just don't do it that way.

Include is itself a process. And the way we implement it is by what I call the Five I's:

Invite

Input

Include

Involve

Invest

Briefly put, what the Five I's mean is that you Invite people to participate, you then solicit and gather information and take seriously their Input, you Include them in the decision making, you Involve them in the implementation, and when all of that happens you will have made them feel genuinely Invested in the business.

Include is sort of the fulcrum of the process, the key juncture at which you have made everyone in the business feel essential. Because we work at it, the Five I's process has become an integral part of our culture, and hopefully it shows up in almost everything we do.

One telltale sign is that we rarely make a unilateral decision, but rather have everyone feel like part of the steps that lead to a decision. After all, a unilateral decision springs from the distasteful notion that since my name is on this door, do as I say. The only time I can remember making a unilateral decision is when there was a fire at one of our stores. "Get out of the building, there's a fire!" I said early one Saturday morning. "This is not a test!"

And I suppose Scott Mitchell issued something of a unilateral decision when he recently sent around the message: "Please do not put ANY drinks in the top section of the minifridges—they explode!"

Other than to save lives or soda, though, we don't go in for old-fashioned orders.

In the earlier days of our business, after Mom and Dad passed the torch and there were just two Mitchells, Bill and myself, we just wouldn't do something unless we both agreed. In fact, I recall that Bill and I used to rely on the buzzword *strongly*—if one of us *strongly* disagreed with the other, we just didn't do it. It evolved into, All right, I respect Bill more in this area so I'll go along with and really support this new initiative that Bill proposed, or vice versa. But if one of us couldn't make that commitment, we just didn't do it, and I dare say it is very similar today with ten Mitchells in the business.

The purpose of the Five I's is to achieve "buy-in," to create a win-win situation and generate a positive and exciting consensus with those who are connected with the meeting, project, purpose, or cause. That way, at the end of the process people are united as a team charging off to win the game and the Super Bowl. I used to call it the consensus process, my leadership style.

The Five I's are not theoretical baloney. Many of the very best ideas really do come from our own people—all of our people. And they're the ones who have to execute the ideas. When they're included, they become excited and enthusiastic, and then they execute with conviction and consistency. They thirst for success, because they feel invested in that success. Like the other principles, it's common sense.

If a company continuously includes its people in almost everything they want to be included in, then they feel terrific. I think of it as making many into one.

Because you can't do it alone!

Now let me describe how the Five I's work.

CHAPTER 23

Invite

It's hard to feel included in something if you haven't been invited to become part of it. Until you're invited, you're an outsider. And so this is where the process starts.

But whom do you invite and how do you invite them? It shouldn't be done in a slapdash manner, but in a thoughtful way.

Now, there's a huge hug challenge here, because, much as you might like to, you can't invite everyone to everything—every meeting, every strategy session, every celebration. So you don't. But you do keep the door open so that if the buying department has a good idea for sales or selling, they feel comfortable and free to express it, and vice versa.

The people you do invite are everyone whose input you believe could add value to the issue at hand. And that means people who are most *informed* about the matter under exploration. In most instances, obviously, uninformed people aren't going to contribute much value. It's also essential that these colleagues will be extremely comfortable giving their candid opinions in a constructive manner, whether it's positive or negative. People who are crucial to a program's long-range success, if it comes to fruition, are invited even when we know they might offer a knee-jerk negative view of the idea or program we are talking about.

The broader the issue being contemplated—sellers' compensation, for instance, affects all sellers; a major expansion would touch everyone—the more people you invite, because more people are going to be affected by the ultimate decision. And often there's an interim step of "testing the waters," when you invite a small group to float an idea, and if the feedback you get is that it's a bad idea you may scrap it before inviting a larger group to consider it.

And always, always try to have a written agenda that states the purpose of the meeting. That allows people to come prepared. And don't forget to put "Reconnect" on the agenda too!

TRY FOUR PLUS ONE

A technique we've used very effectively—not for every meeting, but at some of them—is known as Four Plus One. It's when you make an exception to the notion of not inviting uninformed people. David Bork is a big advocate of it, and he's brought great clarity to the concept. It works like this: at meetings, you split up into groups of four people, all of whom are knowledgeable on an issue, and then add one more—the "plus one"—who knows nothing, or next to nothing, about the matter but who might add something useful.

For instance, I'd love to inject Todd Bonner, our capable controller, into a group exploring new fashion collections and how to look for and discover them. Why do this? Since he doesn't have his ego invested in the subject, he might spark the best ideas by asking out-of-the-box questions—simple, seemingly stupid but great questions like "Hey, why do you guys do it this way?" That, in turn, makes the others think in fresh ways, and you may get some wonderful new ideas.

David, in fact, claims that studies have established that groups that contain this "plus one" are far more productive and creative than all-expert groups.

Sometimes, but rarely, you might invite someone you know will feel slighted if he isn't invited, even though he isn't that informed and you think he might even slightly inhibit the process. Why? To motivate that person, especially if it's a key individual. Have you ever been overlooked for a meeting that you felt you could have made a contribution to? I have, and I know I felt excluded and lonely. When I'm invited and I can't be there in person, I will call in and participate. Chris Mitchell, who's often in our Long Island store when we are meeting in Connecticut, does this, too, and we think it's a good idea to rely on the telephone and on video conferencing when many miles separate the participants.

When you invite someone, there are various ways you can do it. We believe that the more *personal* the invitation the better. Of course, with large gatherings, it may appear hard to personalize the invitation, but in most cases it is easily done and very effective. Almost always the order of personalization is *in person, handwritten note using a real pen, phone call, voice mail, then e-mail.*

Now, you also need to know what's most appropriate for the people you're inviting, depending on who they are and their preference for receiving communications. For me, if I'm inviting Arthur Levitt, the former commissioner of the SEC, it'll be by a personalized e-mail. If I'm inviting my brother, Bill, it'll be in person, because he would be insulted if I used any of the other methods since I see him so often in the store and socially! If you're the one running an extra-special meeting, and even though your assistant is handling the invitations, try very hard to put your own mark on it. Again, personalization is the point. It shows that you care enough to do it.

It was a huge "invite" hug when Bob Mitchell asked Tullio, our head tailor at Richards, to go to Italy when we began our private label clothing business. It was a way to solicit Tullio's advice and council on the workmanship in these manufacturing plants. Domenic, who holds a similar position at Mitchells, quietly said that he wasn't interested, although he appreciated being invited. I believe Dom would have felt excluded if we had not invited him.

But I say invite, invite, invite, and if the person does not want to come—whether we're talking about the head tailor or the North Koreans—at least you gave them a shot. You told them that they're important to the issue at hand, so then they won't feel excluded.

One other thing that we like to do is the unexpected invitation. It's sort of a twist on the Four Plus One method. Now and then, we'll invite someone to a meeting who wouldn't normally be invited. The idea is not so much that the person's input is needed—though it may well prove valuable—but the invitation makes the person feels great, and we love making people feel great.

For instance, *MR* magazine ("The Magazine of Menswear Retailing") gets some of its best ideas from interns who are encouraged to contribute at the weekly editorial meetings. These college students work without pay, but because they are made to feel important they are comfortable sharing and come up with some great out-of-the-box concepts.

Once we invited Sandra, our receptionist–telephone operator at Mitchells, to speak at a hugging circle (a meeting of associates we set up so they could share positive stories and experiences in our stores), and she was thrilled to be invited. I was surprised and simply delighted when she shared how she plays the "good morning game." She had noticed that as our associates checked in on the computer in the morning, right in front of her, that several never said good morning. So she became proactive and very emphatically said good morning to them, even when she got no response, until eventually she hit 100 percent and everyone started exchanging a smile and a good morning with her. We wouldn't have known all that if we hadn't invited her.

And soon thereafter we gave her the well-deserved title of director of first impressions. She loved it, and immediately ordered new business cards.

CHAPTER 24

Input

It warmed my heart when I read recently that SAS Institute, a software company in North Carolina, had a town hall meeting of its associates and some of the questions that were asked came from a landscaper. That wouldn't happen at most companies. For one thing, the landscaper wouldn't even have been at the meeting—he would have been out trimming hedges and spreading fertilizer—and if he had wandered in, he surely wouldn't have had the courage to say anything. But SAS management, which I understand works hard at hugging its associates, enables *everyone* to feel equal and so *everyone* feels comfortable speaking up.

That's what we believe in so firmly. It's not enough to just invite people to meetings. You need to pick their brains *and* actually listen to what they say, not just let them talk while you daydream and doodle. At many companies, the leaders and managers don't ask their people, or hardly ever ask them, for advice or suggestions or reactions to strategies—even when they're sitting across from them in a meeting. After a while, people, in effect, "lose" their voices. They're either afraid to give their opinions or they don't bother because they know it's a waste of time. And thus you've silenced your greatest reservoir of ideas and information.

For people to feel *accountable* for the behavior of a company, every voice has to have the opportunity to be heard. Every voice, not just the voices of the bigwigs.

The majority of companies, it seems to us, fail to listen to associates when making even the most minor decisions—like what color to repaint the associate bathrooms. I've heard that managers order supplies or equipment without once consulting the people who will be using the equipment. They'll purchase new computers or software or desk chairs or even trucks, and just spring the stuff on their associates. Maybe some drivers wanted a green truck rather than a blue truck, and it wouldn't have cost any more to have gotten a green truck or to have asked the drivers in the first place.

Gosh, one of the simplest and easiest ways to make people feel part of the team is to *ask* up front for their input. In our view, it's also very important how you ask. Two great remarks I've learned over the years to get your huggers to share genuine input are:

1. "I need your help, Norberto," or even stronger, "Norberto, I really need your help," on whatever the topic is.

2. "What do you think?" Or "Mark, what do you think?" Dad's habit, after making a declarative statement, was to say, "The Red Sox (or the Yankees) stink, don't you think?" (Or the one I love the most, Dad's great phrase regarding Bill: "Bill has a way of making people feel good, don't you think?")

So "I really need your help" and "What do you think?" are ideal ways to tell huggers that not only do you want their input but you actually value it and will consider it.

When gathering advice, try to stay focused on the mission or purpose of the project. (Occasionally, though, you get a brilliant idea that might apply to another area within your business.) And being sincerely open to input means that you have to be willing to invite disagreement. You shouldn't in any way frown on or, heaven forbid, punish people for having differences of opinion. I always say to myself, and sometimes out loud in a meeting, "No idea is a bad idea. Get it out, share it." I do my best to compliment people who have the confidence to throw out creative, off-the-chart ideas during a meeting. Yet it is important to come back to the central focus of the meeting and at the end prioritize the best ideas of the group that have the greatest chance for success.

For sure, try to give a hug to all the people who give you input—recognition, rewards, and, most of all, sincere appreciation. Some companies value input by awarding cash bonuses or plaques for the best idea of the month. Best of all, to our mind, is to offer genuine thanks before one's peers and to demonstrate true interest.

One day at Marshs Mary shared with us that it used to drive her crazy when her former manager in her previous job would pick her brains and then the next day steal credit for Mary's input. What a punch in the face that was—and the opposite of a hug!

When it's appropriate, it makes people feel good when you act right away on their input. When we acquired Richards, we immediately solicited input from the associates about any changes that interested them—or, for that matter, lack of changes. One young man stuck up his hand and said, "I hope you're not going to change the softball team!" I said, "Of course, we all want the softball team—right?" Hands went up. Then someone said, "We really need shoes here, we need to service our customers." You see, Richards had the finest collection of men's clothing, sportswear, and furnishings, but— would you believe it?—no shoes! So I said, "Who'd like shoes here?" Every hand shot up. I turned to Bob Mitchell, and said, "Let's get some shoes in here. Let's service our customers from head to toe, and cover those toes, too!" Within two weeks, Richards was selling shoes. So, just like that, input on the softball team and shoes was easily addressed.

Of course, it gets ticklish and sort of tricky when you don't accept somebody's advice, because she might feel that you don't respect her or you were just going through the motions. But all you need to do is explain to her that you've gone in another direction and candidly let her know that it's not personal and that you will continue to solicit her input on future matters. Then clearly elaborate on the value of the idea you selected and why it will have a better chance of success. People appreciate the candor and often thank you for simply incorporating them in the decision-making process—it's a hug.

A common way that many businesses gather input is through suggestion boxes. I don't like them. To me, they symbolize an impersonal way to communicate and they send the message that the senior staff is too lazy to take the time to sit down and listen to a new idea or a complaint, or is even afraid to go face-to-face with their people. We'd rather have the offices of our leaders or managers be the suggestion boxes. Or any place in the store—the men's room, the dressing room, the shoe stockroom. Simply walk in and say straight away what's on your mind. We're all arms, eyes, and ears.

CHAPTER 25

Include

It always sort of surprised and frustrated me when Dad used to tell me in no uncertain terms that I was indecisive and couldn't make a quick decision. When something had to be decided, I would often say—and I remember it drove Dad nuts—"Let's sleep on the idea, let's get some more input."

Sleeping on it was sometimes my way of saying, "Dad, let's include some others so they feel it's their decision too."

I would literally sleep on it so that we made absolutely sure that the decision we came up with was the right thing to do. I've always found that if you take your decision to bed with you, then when the sun rises the next day and you feel great about that decision—your right brain and left brain are connected—you can go for it and execute it. Or you often say, "Ya know, I really need to include one or two other people in this decision-making process. Perhaps they will modify the idea a touch, or maybe just having them be aware of all of the thinking that has gone into this will make them feel included."

I used to call it consensus leadership.

See, I was simply following the Five I's.

Include means that after you've invited associates and gathered their input, you allow them to participate in assessing that input and making a decision based on it. I guess what agitated Dad was that it seemed to him that by sleeping on something so we could include others it was slowing down the process. Well, actually the opposite is true. It speeds it up.

We can act more quickly and decisively if all agree on an action. I call it a "no-brainer"!

So when everyone at Richards agreed we needed shoes, we said what they say at Nike: "Just do it." And I added, "Let's get on with it!"

Most projects and programs take time. They just do. By waiting to get as much "buy-in" as possible, though, usually a far better resolution comes about. *Resolution* is a big word. I always say you never, or rarely, *solve* any issue, not in today's fast-changing world, but you can *resolve* it. And resolution means taking the time to explain the issue and why you feel the way you do to others.

The other thing is, when you make a decision without involving a broad enough constituency, there's bound to be some resistance from those who don't agree with it, as well as apathy from those who might concur but were unhappy about not being consulted. This resistance drastically slows the implementation of the idea. It can often doom it.

It's clear to us that decisions that don't include associates fail more often than they succeed. Those that do include them succeed the vast majority of the time. If you include your associates, you never—or almost never—get surprises, and you achieve consistency of execution and attain a much higher degree of success because you get everyone reading from the same page.

When we bought Richards, for instance, I was strongly in favor of changing the name to Mitchells. I invited input from our advisory board. Pretty much everyone disagreed with me, especially members of the Mitchell family. I "slept on it," weighing what they shared, and soon saw the wisdom in keeping the Richards name. We retained the equity of a great local brand name, Richards, that for almost fifty years had been near and dear to the hearts of the Greenwich people, especially the associates. I've never regretted it. It was the right decision.

So often I've heard laments like this from friends or customers about their company: "They hired this guy and didn't tell me or ask my opinion or let me meet him before we hired him, and I have to work with him. It made me feel like a nobody."

It would be so much better when you're contemplating hiring someone to share his résumé with those who will work directly with him and then to take him around and introduce him and let them get to know him a bit. Later, ask their opinions before making a decision. Then everyone feels included, even the new hire.

It's very powerful that our buyers—let's select my lovely wife,

Linda, as an example—include the sales associates in the buying process, and they love it! When Linda goes on a major buy in Paris or Milan, she returns with pictures and descriptions of what she has seen and is *considering* (that's the key word) buying. And she goes to Richards and reviews all of these pictures and asks, What do you think, Jacquie? What do you think, AnneMarie, will Vanna or Barbara buy it? It's a huge hug to be recognized as experts and feel genuinely invited, listened to, and included in the buying decision. Clearly Linda writes the order and doesn't always follow their advice. That's why she's the buyer and they're the sellers. But she genuinely includes them—and so hugs them.

And when a new season approaches, the buyers have a "trend meeting," one for men's and one for women's fashions. The sales force is expected to attend, and anyone is invited to hear the perspective of our buying team on how they see fashion trends for fall or spring. One thing we sometimes do at the men's sessions is divide the sales associates into teams to put outfits together—tie, shirt, suit, shoes—and then everyone quickly votes on the "best" ones. It gets the sellers and buyers involved in thinking about new combinations from the new inventory.

Bill and I were very proud of Bob Mitchell, who made the final decision when we recently moved from a commission to a noncommission system for our sellers at Mitchells. The switch was after much thought, many small group meetings, sessions with the women's department and men's department, plus one-on-one's with Todd Mitchell, Mitchells store manager Tom

Maleri, and team leader Trish Kaylor. Bob and Todd and, of course, Bill spent endless hours at men's and women's meetings that included everyone, from veteran sellers of many years to the new rising stars. We got almost unanimous buy-in from owners to sales managers to sales associates, because it was a great plan and we included them. Russ did a terrific Power-Point presentation for a meeting he led with the Mitchells sales force prior to the change in compensation, and then the first week they received their paychecks under the new system he entertained questions and made sure everyone continued to feel included.

Three weeks afterward, Bob received an e-mail from Joe DeRosa, a wonderful men's sales associate who has been with us at Mitchells for twelve years: "I was thinking of retiring at seventy. With this new system, I think I'll be around until at least seventy-five."

CUDDLE IN THE HUDDLE

A critical way to include people is by forming teams. But we mean teams where there's genuine sharing and everyone participates in decisions. After we visited Harry Rosen's store in Canada a number of years ago and saw the wonderful use of teams there, Bob Mitchell divided our sales associates into teams. We have five to eight people assigned to each unit, along with a team leader. Note that we call them leaders, as opposed to team managers or supervisors. Rather than be a dictator, we want them to lead or coach in a way that is democratic, allowing the sales associates to grow and have fun working to service clients in their own unique way.

I'm the team captain at Richards, Bob's the captain at Mitchells, and Chris is the captain at Marshs. We have weekly round-table meetings where we reconnect and listen and learn together, always trying to raise the bar. We discuss each associate who needs some positive assistance or coaching—we try to focus on what each associate is positively doing in the selling process and how we can have other sellers pick up on their positive strengths to improve everyone's performance. And then the team leaders meet as often as possible with the individual sales associates in an informal and sometimes formal way to check in on them, see how they're doing. And where there are areas that need improvement or where they can grow, team leaders give them suggestions.

Once a month, the three stores' team leaders meet, using an agenda set by Bob, who always invites team leaders to put anything they wish on the agenda so they feel included. After using this format for a while, Bob enlarged the conference table, and a portion of the meeting now includes people from other departments like visual, buying, and marketing/advertising. That's a company-wide people culture!

A very similar system operates with our buying team. At least once a month, all the buyers meet with Bob, our merchant, and Russ, the financial man, to discuss buying strategy and planning.

Our friend Howard Vogt from Rodes, a great clothing store in Louisville, has his huggers assemble in a huddle every day, just like a sports team. The women have been saying that it's time to "cuddle in our huddle." It's a great way for a team to bond. I love it!

And Steve Anderson, my consulting dentist friend, suggests to his cadre of dentists a similar type of huddle every morning in their offices to review the patients they will see that day. Not only do they discuss the crowns and root canals to be performed, but also the personal preferences of each customer. Steve, like Howard, has shared with us that this helps to build a wonderful team. As they do at our stores, the clients feel the team spirit, too—that's the hugging culture!

We're strong advocates of team-building exercises, and it's wise to use a facilitator to help out. At the Wilton YMCA, our family council has done rope and wall climbing, as well as wire treetop sliding, where everyone waits for you at the bottom and gives you a hug. Many times, I've gone to sleep at night dreaming of the time I saw Linda (like Jane in *Tarzan*, except Linda wore a harness) jumping off a platform suspended from a tree and being hugged by all of us once she reached the bottom. And we have also done an outdoor scavenger hunt. As I recall, it was the first time I've ever laughed so hard with Sue Mitchell, Bill's wife. We had to use compasses and other mechanical devices that required analytic skills. We've also done some cooking classes together, splitting up into teams to make Asian dishes or Italian food. There's nothing like bonding over a great lasagna.

On another occasion, we came up with questions for the team members to answer. One of them was "What one word describes you?" I clearly remember that Karen, Bob's wife, used the word *tenacious* for me and I had to agree. Then I in turn told her I believe she is tenacious also. We laughed heartily about that.

Many times at meetings of the women's department sales associates at Mitchells run by Scott, he will invite one of the team members to lead the meeting in his place. It's a small thing, but that person feels included and great inside.

When you conduct your meetings, don't forget to have them in a circle or at a round table, if possible, so people face one another and no one looms at the head of the table. It's an important signal of inclusion. I call it the Power of the Round Table or the Hugging Circle. It's *so* much more powerful in the sharing and synergy of ideas, and it makes people feel that the playing field is level. They are more comfortable speaking up rather than expecting to be lectured to. I hear about meetings at other companies where participants have to raise their hands if they need to go to the bathroom. They've got to be kidding!

THE PRICE OF EXCLUSION

Now, I should point out that sometimes you need to keep issues or plans private, and this is where a culture of *trust* intersects with the wish to *include.* Indeed, we learned this years ago when we fouled up the deal to buy Richards by including too many people. Since we were dealing with a different leadership style and a father-daughter team to boot, they felt overwhelmed and the talks collapsed. So when we revisited this in 1994, Bob and I alone negotiated with Eddie and Susan, their leaders, because we now knew that in this situation it was vital to have no more than a "two-on-two."

But this should happen only on rare occasions. Because while the cost of exclusion can't be measured in dollars and cents, it's huge. It's bigger than you think. It starts smaller than you think.

Let me tell you a story that happened to me. It didn't seem like a big deal. In fact, I was surprised at my own reaction. It was just a dinner involving some of the top sellers to celebrate their stellar performances. In the past, I had been invited along. In this instance, I wasn't. When I heard that the dinner was happening without me—"It's a generational thing," I was told—I was crushed. It was winter and that night I took a walk around the block, in the bitter cold, trying to sort out why I felt so dispirited. I couldn't sleep that night. I actually wrote down some of the words and phrases that captured my emotions: I feel awful, I feel alone, huge demotivator, sad, empty, down, has anyone asked what motivates me? I'm thinking: I'm old fast.

At many companies someone would just brood and wallow in his bruised feelings. We're an open culture, and so I expressed my pain to the person in charge of the dinner. He told me that he appreciated my sharing my reaction. He acknowledged my feelings and said he was sorry that I felt this way. But he added that I was making too much out of something and should "get over it. Let it go."

And I felt better and let it go. And then one day, lo and behold, suddenly I was invited and included in the next dinner. It felt good. And after the dinner I felt great!

You can't deny other people's feelings. I'm going to say that again to emphasize a life-long lesson: you can't deny other people's feelings. Their feelings are very real. Listen and acknowledge them: "I hear you. You felt excluded"—or underappreciated or whatever. It doesn't matter if someone *shouldn't* make too much of something if he *did* make a lot of something. After all, they're *his* feelings.

And so the message got sent that something like this is a big motivator for me, and that ought to be respected in the future.

At most companies, I'll bet if you asked people to write down ten occasions when they felt included in a business decision and ten times that they felt excluded, they wouldn't be able to fill the first list and they'd run out of space for the second.

Go try it now.

Ask a few people chosen at random, and brace yourself for their responses.

And listen.

CHAPTER 26

Involve

Once decisions are made, you need to call on everyone who is affected by them to implement them, and that could be a particular department or it could be the entire company. The best strategies in the world are worthless if they aren't effectively and consistently carried out—"executed," as Larry Bossidy, who wrote the book *Execution,* would say. And so this is where you have to *involve* people.

If you've followed the Five I's thus far, then you will have had significant buy-in to the decision, because you've invited the right people, used their input, and included them in the decision making. I used to call this strategy "win-win," and it still fits. So implementing the decision should be smooth and effective, because unlike in companies that don't use this process, it's not an order that comes out of the blue but is a mutually agreed-upon action. It's not what people are told to do, but what they want to do, because they've decided themselves that they want to do it.

But, depending on the action, far more people generally haven't been included than have. So you need to draw them into the process by involving them so they can carry it out. We strongly believe that no one is going to be committed to something without being involved.

The key here is communication. Open, honest communication, so sorely lacking in business, is very much the backbone of the Five I's. When Bob Mitchell came into the family business more than fifteen years ago, he very clearly and directly said to Bill and me, "The only thing that could take us down is lack of or poor communication." That really made an impression on us—we obviously never forgot it—and it may be one of the reasons we try to go overboard and keep everyone informed, because we believe bone-deep that Bob is correct.

The operative philosophy at many businesses is to communicate to their associates strictly on a need-to-know basis, and what that usually translates to is as little information as possible. Sometimes it's no information at all, but simply a set of commands. This often creates a divide-and-conquer mentality. Companies will announce, "Starting tomorrow, we're eliminating the lunch hour, so try to eat a hearty breakfast. Have a good day."

My philosophy has always been to communicate *not* on a *need-to-know* basis but on a *want-to-know* basis. In other words, we tell our people everything they *want to know* about a decision or strategy that is relevant to their business success—and then some. The extra is a hug so that they fully understand the *value* of what it means, why it's happening, and how it will affect them. That way they will become involved in carrying it out.

What associates want to know is usually a great deal more than management thinks they need to know. There's an easy way to find out. You ask them. My perspective often is that we give "too much" information, but that's okay, because we'd rather give too much than too little. We keep communicating and communicating until associates and managers say, as Jeff likes to say, either verbally or nonverbally, "All right already, enough is enough, I get it!"

It's always better this way. People have a tendency to overreact to incomplete or ambiguous information. You see this all the time during wild swings in the stock market: someone whispers that a key world leader is ill and people imagine he's on his deathbed and fear massive disruption and so the markets panic, when all he actually has is a hangnail on his ring finger. So you need to get as much accurate information out as possible, clearly presented.

After decisions are made, we engage in ample amounts of both in-person and written communications that are open and honest. Associates quickly see through distortions and "spin," so don't insult them with phony information. And managers, as well as all the people who were included in making the decision, should be available for any questions that the formal communications don't answer.

And then you need to do continual follow-up on a formal and informal basis to see that everyone understands what has been decided.

Sometimes you find that people are unhappy with a strategy. Despite all the inclusion you arranged, you may have misjudged how it would go over. So then you tweak it or, in some instances, even reverse it. That's the ultimate signal to your associates that they are important to the process and have been heard. Even after a decision has been made, and it's a mistake, you will change it. It shows you have respect for them.

When you communicate fully and honestly and effectively, associates are able to do their jobs better and carry out new strategies effectively so that everyone wins. And they feel very, very involved.

CHAPTER 27

Invest

Now you've reached the culmination of the Five I's process, and here's where you really witness a terrific payoff. People feel *invested,* which is a marvelous feeling indeed.

What does this signify? Well, when people have participated in a meaningful way in the process through the other four I's—Invite, Input, Include, Involve—they come to feel *ownership,* even if only in a tiny way. What you're doing, in effect, is *creating* a feeling of ownership without *ceding* ownership. There are two types of ownership in a business—legal ownership, when the associates actually possess stock in the company, and the sense of ownership, when people are granted the power to behave as if they are owners. Often, the latter can be as strong or stronger as the former.

Among other things, it is so much easier to communicate with passion and have the ability to execute when everyone feels ownership. And it's common sense that invested associates feel better about themselves than uninvested ones. They work harder. They're happier. And they're a lot more loyal.

When we bought Marshs a few years ago, we followed the Five I's to the letter, and it made for an exciting process and a very smooth transition.

As we were finalizing terms with Ron Marsh and his family, they decided to invite Sue Gilbert (who had worked with the Marsh family for more than twenty years and was regarded almost as a family member) into the discussions about our buying their family business. At various times before the papers were signed, they also informed Steve Kerman (who has worked for Marshs for more than thirty years and whose father worked for Marshs before him) and Tony Famiglietti (who was another valued long-term sales associate). Before we signed the documents to buy the business, we also had the opportunity to confidentially speak to Sue, Steve, and Tony, which made them feel so much more included and invested in the success of the merger.

When we gathered input from Ron, Sue, Steve, and Tony, they were open enough to share with us that there were communication challenges among the huggers on the selling floor. Associates trusted the Marsh family and felt they were great people, but they really didn't love getting up and coming to work every day, because the compensation system and physical layout of the store were poor. Poor is an understatement. Without rehashing the challenges, the atmosphere had deteriorated to the point where some associates hadn't talked to each other in years and they were crying out for a change.

In fact, the Marshes were planning to address these issues prior to the negotiations with us. They were wise. Wise enough to understand that they didn't have the answers to solve these challenges and wise enough to wait until both families could work together with the associates to resolve the issues.

When we made the announcement to the entire Marshs team that we had merged, we deliberately included Frank, John, and Jeff, three of our top Richards sales associates. Why? Because the same thing had happened to them ten years earlier when we bought Richards, and they could honestly confirm that their lives had improved dramatically since the merger with Mitchells. I remember John saying something like "Believe me, you guys have just hit the trifecta! Trust the Mitchells. Your lives will be so much better and you'll have more fun! It's been like that for me and all the veterans at Richards."

Using the word *merger* rather than *acquire* in the announcement was a huge hug to the associates because it softened the relationship. *Acquire* or *sold* would have made them feel like pawns in a chess game. Afterward, we all went out to dinner and we began to hug as a team.

Meanwhile, we began to gather data on the huggers to listen and learn on a one-on-one basis the positive strengths of each member of the Marshs team—be they sales associates, tailors, or in shipping and receiving. We then focused them on hugging their customers, and introduced our computer and systems. It became obvious to them that they needed to build *personal relationships* with one another. We explained how to connect and reconnect. In due course, people begin to share things like "I visited my grandchildren yesterday," "I love extra-chunky peanut butter," "I hate *The Sopranos*." Colleagues learned that Gerry likes the Yankees, Steve has a son named Sam who is the light of his life, Colleen and Sue love to party in Montauk, and all of a sudden a hug-your-people environment blossomed. We even had a company-wide surprise hugging contest where we gave associates a financial hug if they achieved a goal and they achieved it together.

We invited everyone's input on how we could improve things. We devised a new compensation system, where everyone could sell anything by "playing" as a team. And we renovated the store, using input from associates on how to configure the layout so they could better service customers. They began to "get" that we really wanted them to feel included.

I began to physically hug certain huggers who wanted a hug. Others got a high five, a personalized thank-you note, or a telephone call or e-mail, or all of these. And it just wasn't me, it was Chris and Bob and Russ and Linda Mitchell and Lisa Coppotelli, Bob's merchandising assistant. When Lisa brought her team from Mitchells and Richards over to reticket something like twenty-four thousand items and she began to ask for help, everyone felt included and the connecting began to happen between the three stores big-time. The same thing occurred when Tony Gregario came over to show Will Daley how Tony had set up the Mitchells shipping and receiving department.

One by one, the associates started to care for one another again, or maybe for the first time, talking to one another not only on a professional basis but on a *personal* basis: "Robin, you have such great taste, could you help me pick out a present for my husband for our anniversary? It's a big one."

They never had meetings before. Now people began to look *forward* to meetings. In the past, they never knew the sales goal for the day, only their individual sales, and had no idea how the business was doing. And that, along with everything else, kept them from feeling invested. Now that a certain part of their pay is based on store sales, everyone checks the computer often to see the sales score. Are we in the seventh inning? Do we have time for a stretch and some peanuts, or should we keep selling with intensity and focus, using all of us to win the day? They know the score in this open culture.

Fast-forward to today. Marshs has become a new world. I'm so proud of Chris Mitchell and Ron Marsh and everyone else who put so much time into helping create the change. It may not be a perfect new world, but there has been a fundamental paradigm shift where associates are literally and figuratively hugging one another. It's very exciting to see.

Tony and Steve actually hugged each other Christmas Eve. Tony, using the "Italian hug," gave Steve a kiss on the cheek on New Year's Eve. Wow! As I went to sleep after learning about these hugs from Chris, I felt absolutely fantastic.

As my friends at CCA Global Partners, an $8 billion business, said, "It's the power of all of us!"

I say it a dash differently: "The Five I's (Invite, Input, Include, Involve, Invest) is a powerful process that enables everyone to play together."

HUGGING STUDY GUIDE #4

INCLUDE

You can't do it alone: So don't try. Make sure that everyone feels included in decision making and strategy by following the Five I's, a five-step process that gets everyone playing the game together.

Invite: Don't just invite people to make decisions randomly but choose those who are informed about the issue at hand. Use the preferred means of inviting them: in person, by handwritten note, by voice mail, or by e-mail—and be as personal as possible.

Input: Seek real input from everyone, including the landscaper, not just the bigwigs. And make it clear that you intend to use it. The best way to gather input about a particular issue is by saying, "I need your help" or "What do you think?"

Include: Allow the people you've invited input from to actually participate in the decision making. Set up teams with leaders who act like members, go out and cook lasagna or Chinese together, and at meetings sit in circles so no one dominates.

Involve: To inspire associates to carry out decisions and strategy, you need open and honest communication, and you have to tell people not what you think they *need to know* but what they *want to know*. How do you find out? Ask them.

Invest: The culmination of the process is that people feel invested. They have the sense of ownership, even if they haven't been ceded ownership.

PART FIVE

Recognize

It's Not Only About Money

CHAPTER 28

But Don't Forget Money

If people are Nice, Trusted, Proud, and Included, then the Recognition will certainly follow. And that doesn't mean strictly dollars and cents.

Our strong feeling is that money is not the main reason people choose where they work for life—for a career. After all, money can't compensate for your boss's ignoring you and it surely can't cancel out having to work beside boorish and ill-mannered colleagues. That's why people say of an offensive boss, "I wouldn't work with him for a million bucks." And so we don't believe in a money-rules-the-day mentality.

At the same time, however, if the money and the fringe benefits are not commensurate with the job performance—and then some—in the context of the local market and the living standards in the community, then associates feel "used" or that the owners and management are "chintzy" and just raking in the bucks for themselves.

We believe that if you don't pay people enough, it negates everything else—all the other four principles. So money is sort of a wild card. I insist that I don't work only for the money—and I do believe this—yet if I were not recognized or rewarded fairly within our business, I wouldn't have the passion that I have to do what I do.

When people go home to share with their families, at the end of the day they want to arrive with a smile and with a good feeling and with a wallet that is filled with enough, or in many cases more than enough, to make them believe that the investment that they have made of their time, energy, and talent has been recognized and recognized a lot. Especially when the associates can see that the business—in our case, the stores—currently are doing so well.

Therefore you can't forget money.

My feeling has always been very straightforward. I like to pay our people very well—extremely well. Of course, you have to be realistic and stick within the financial parameters and playing field of your business and industry. The expectations have to be set accordingly. I believe all associates should feel that they have the opportunity to earn more if they hit their goals and the stores hit their goals, and if they are constantly raising the bar and becoming better.

The way we operate most of the time is we pay associates more to start than they were earning elsewhere. That immediately makes them feel great. Since we have fewer people than our competitors of equivalent size—but great people—they produce more, and that enables us to pay them more each year. So far this has worked well. Every time I've compared our numbers to the few industry studies I've seen of sales divided by total associates, we have the most productive ratio by far.

At performance review time, most of our associates are extremely satisfied, which naturally makes us feel pleased. Now and then, a few are disappointed, and so we listen and explain and reset goals and expectations.

We've had only one *really* tough time, from 1989 to 1991, when we were forced to freeze wages and eliminate bonuses. I remember during a tailor shop meeting explaining why no one was getting raises or bonuses. Vicki Batsu, one of our valued tailors, spoke up with conviction and emotion: "Jack, we all understand. We're lucky to have a job. We trust you and your family. We recognize that when times get better we'll not only have a job but we will move forward again." When I think back on those years, our associates understood and they applauded our prudent moves because we had invested in them. We strongly believe that if we have a downturn tomorrow, the vast majority of our team will be just as supportive as they were during that turbulent period.

Besides salary, you ought to incorporate occasional incentive programs and consider giving people discretionary bonuses from time to time. We sometimes bestow a certificate for a dinner or a round of golf, or else tickets to a sports events or Broadway show—again, we make a concerted effort to be sure these are rewards aligned to the beneficiary's passions.

In addition, we have a defined bonus plan for some areas within the store, such as the buying team. A certain portion of their bonus is based on measurable factors like gross profit and turn rate.

We have created programs like the 2-4-6-8 bonus program, which includes everyone from the stores (except the family). We started it after 9/11, when people were understandably feeling gloomy and full of uncertainty. It works like this: from November 10 to Christmas, if there's a 2 percent increase in sales over a year ago, everyone gets a bonus of "x" amount—say $250. If sales rise 4 percent, they get double that, or $500, and so on up the ladder. Everyone gets the bonus. Tailors get it, buyers get it, receptionists get it, parking attendants get it, everyone. That way, it inspires teamwork throughout the entire organization.

Sophia at Richards has been known to jump up onto the counter and belt out exuberant cheers like "Let's go, let's go—two, four, six, eight, who do we appreciate . . . Rickee, Nadia, Nina, yeahhhh!"

We find that when all of our associates "work for the customer," they work with one another even better. It's fabulous because it creates a level playing field where everybody wins when the store wins, not just the sellers.

I call it a *company-wide associate-and-customer-centric hugging culture.*

This magic does indeed pay off. In a study of more than two thousand businesses, the Gallup Organization found that sales were 3.4 times higher when engaged associates sold to engaged customers.

These bonus periods are marvelous things to behold. And remember we do them during the busiest and most profitable time of the year.

We also really like short-term contests. For instance, we might hold one where the purpose is for our sellers to focus for a prescribed period of time on one product or collection, such as the number of made-to-measure men's orders for a Zegna or Brioni weekend trunk show. We also engage in slightly lengthier contests—if we sell 70 percent of our Armani Collezioni stock for the season, incentives will be awarded.

Because we don't have assigned parking spots, one piece of recognition we sometimes give for contest winners at Mitchells is the right to park in "choice" parking spots close to the associates' entrance for a defined time. Goodness, is that a treasured benefit when it's five below outside.

A valuable by-product of contests is that associates learn a lot about a product or department, which helps them perform not only in the short run but also in the long run once the contest ends. We try hard to set up these events so at least everyone has an opportunity to win, which means you sometimes have to handicap people just like you do in golf, so you don't constantly have the same winners. What happens, of course, is that even if you handicap a Frank Gallagi or an Amy Jarman, they're so extraordinary that they just sell more! So you have to keep giving everyone else more strokes.

As we are all aware, one of the dangers of contests is that associates might sell a product only when there's a contest going. This scenario happens infrequently, but it does happen. When we detect this behavior, we remind everyone that we need to focus on what's best for the customer, not what's best to win the contest.

If you're not careful, a contest can sometimes drift into a non-hugging situation if the attitude prevails that there are only winners and losers. Therefore, when we introduce a new contest we always emphasize how the individual members all win by competing against their own goals and not one another. Our huggers usually seem to understand that.

One other interesting way to recognize people is to have the associates do some of the recognizing. I've heard of a people-friendly engineering consultant business where any associate who thinks a colleague has performed exceptionally can award a $50 bonus to the individual right on the spot, without higher approval. Hey, you can bet you're going to like the guy in the next cubicle even better if he puts some extra cash in your pocket!

So try to find a way to pay your people well, and then some.

However, as you will see, we believe associates need a lot more than compensation to motivate them to remain loyal for life.

CHAPTER 29

Run Their Picture, Too

Money takes you part of the way toward recognizing associates and making them feel valued—it does buy *some* happiness—but what else should you do?

Quite a lot.

One of the best ways to recognize people is by creating an experience that they'll never forget. One that I remember from the "old days" that has left a lasting impression and really taught me a lesson sprang entirely from an offhand comment!

You see, in the early 1990s we were just beginning to build our women's department in Westport. Beverly Martin, who was managing that area for us, came to me with a sales plan that she had worked out with Linda. Even I thought it was a real stretch, but what the heck, if Beverly and Linda thought they could do it, I was thrilled.

In an off-the-cuff way, I said, "Ya know, if you hit that number

I'll happily treat you both to a trip to England to buy those antiques I know you love."

And you know what, they did it! And they went! Later on, Bev told me that although she had long respected Linda in a professional way, she had more of an opportunity to get to know her in a personal manner. She also thought it was fantastic because it was a trip tailored to her interests. The mutual respect they developed was evident in the future when Linda invited Bev to Dallas on buying trips. And eventually, they included Jerry, Bev's husband, and me in dinners together, and we became life-long friends!

Luis Sans, a friend and storeowner in Barcelona, was kind enough to share some thoughtful acts of recognition from his business. Back in the 1950s, few people in Spain could enjoy going away for a vacation. So his grandfather made arrangements at a small hotel north of Barcelona so employees could go there for a week, all expenses paid. More recently, the wife of the store manager felt she needed to spend more time with her husband. Luis treated them to a week's trip to Venice. They had the most fantastic time.

Perks that everyone gets are great, and enlightened companies do lots of these. Microsoft offers free grocery delivery and dry cleaning. If you put in five years at Yahoo!, you get a gumball machine, followed by an espresso machine after ten, and a foosball table after fifteen. At Children's Healthcare of Atlanta, one of the amenities they give everyone with a dog or cat (I'm not sure about a llama) is complimentary pet insurance. Adobe Systems has a bocce court.

But what's more meaningful is when you find the thing that means the most to each associate personally and genuinely, and then recognize them by offering them that. If someone is a stickler about their nails, give them weekly manicures for a month. If they're eager to learn bridge, give them bridge lessons.

I got a nice e-mail from a gemologist at WR Chance Diamond Jewelers in Annapolis, Maryland. One month, the team really outdid itself and nearly doubled its monthly goal. Everyone was told there was a sales meeting after work one evening. Bruce Chance, the owner, brought out a bottle of champagne to celebrate, and he gave a really heartwarming speech. The team was thrilled and thought that was that. But Bruce walked them outside to a waiting limo, which took them to Talbots, which had stayed open late just for them. The team was told to go on a shopping spree and pick out an ensemble on the company. You can bet everyone went home feeling on top of the world.

Years ago, we started what we affectionately refer to as million-dollar dinners at Mitchells, when all of a sudden we had several million-dollar sellers—Rita, Phyllis, Paul, and Ray—and it was time to celebrate this accomplishment together with our family members and other senior associates who supported their sales success! We treated them to a great meal and toasted their (then) unbelievable achievement of selling $1 million of merchandise in one year. Today, in all three stores we have more than forty associates who sell more than $1 million annually. Would you believe that several of these great sellers sell more than $2 million, and two sellers last year sold more than $3 million worth of beautiful clothing and accessories!

There are many creative ways that we celebrate success. The other night, Jeff Kozak told me that he took Bruce Kelly, Noella, and Gerry, who all contribute to the success of the men's shoe business at Richards, out to dinner to celebrate achieving selling $2 million of men's shoes. Not long ago, he invited the whole customer service team (ten or so people) to a Mets baseball game.

Simple praise itself goes a long way. When an individual makes a concerted contribution—whether snagging a big sale, consistently waiting on a lot of customers, staying late to ring up an important order or type up a report, or contributing a creative marketing idea that results in a lot of traffic in the store—you should let them know that those acts are greatly appreciated. On Saturday mornings, we hold meetings with various departments before the stores open, and we use them to share "hug" stories that illustrate above and beyond hugging, and thus to recognize associates.

In my weekly CEO letter and e-mail, I love to share stories of extraordinary actions by associates. Here's an example of some praise I received from a sales associate regarding a trend show that I turned around and shared with everyone to multiply the hugs. It was a "twofer"!

Dear all,

This week, we held a women's trend meeting at Mitchells. In attendance were the buying team, tailors, and ladies sellers. All were gathered there to learn about market changes and new collections for all three stores.

And wow! What a wonderful meeting it was! I was so impressed with the professionalism, market knowledge, and teamwork that was shown by all involved! Not only was the meeting itself a great hit, some of the associates were kind enough to share their comments afterward.

Mary wrote this wonderful e-mail that sums up many of the responses:

"Good Morning,

I just wanted to tell you that I was blown away by the trend meeting.

The buying team did an amazing job. I feel that everyone was well prepared and ahead of the trends and very receptive to our feedback.

I felt that they were a solid team working together in a synergistic and very positive way!!!!! Even the tone in which everyone spoke projected confidence. You should be very proud. And Linda's food—the only problem with making such delicious food is topping it next time. Have a wonderful day! Love Mary"

Thank you all for your participation and hugs!

Warm hugs to all,
Jack

And, naturally, managers and even colleagues regularly send letters or e-mails congratulating associates on superior performance.

Sent to all users:
Good day to all,

We would like to take the opportunity to congratulate Theresa Goncalves on her promotion to *Customer Service Manager of Mitchells of Westport.*

Theresa joined us at Mitchells in September 2003 on a part-time basis.

    She has recently assumed full-time status and is now working as the Customer Service Manager.

Please congratulate Theresa in this new endeavor.

Thank you,
Patricia Kaylor

One of the most important points when you hug someone in a letter is who the hug is "copied to." Those cc's at the bottom magnify and multiply the hug, and it's one of the first things an associate looks for. A written hug can always be copied to the person's manager, the department head, and the top person—hey, what the heck, even the owner of the company if it's warranted!

When I personally sign—with a real ink pen—our annual holiday thank-you notes (last year to 1,654 clients), I always mention the women's and men's sales associates that the clients work with. I literally say, "On behalf of all the Mitchells and Debra O'Shea and Ray Cerritelli, we want to thank you for all you have done for us. We wish you a joyous holiday season and super New Year!"

By mentioning the sales associates' names, it's not just me thanking them, it's also Debra and Ray. I've had feedback about how nice it was that I mentioned their names, not only from the customers, but also from Debra and Ray!

We regularly publish "image" books, and especially in our Mitchells/Richards/Marshs magazine that goes out to our customers we make a point of incorporating pictures of our associates or mentioning them by name. When we advertise, we don't get fixated only on fashion models. We've taken individual and group photos of our huggers and included them to recognize them. It's great for their self-confidence to see that we think so highly of them that we advertise them far and wide. Happens every time a new one comes out—like when Linda Gans, one of our jewelry specialists, came up to me and said, "Jack, thanks so much for putting me in the group picture. My daughter was so excited she showed it to all of her friends, made me feel so great!"

What do you think of businesses that feature their people in ads or letters on a regular basis? I've seen more and more companies doing it. It's a nice touch, isn't it? Sort of says they care about their people. A lot.

I've always liked the fact that every time Federal Express puts a new plane into service, it names it after the child of an employee, determined by a drawing. What a great way to recognize people, for you to be able to see the name of your kid inscribed on the nose of a plane. Your kid thinks you're the world's greatest mom or dad, and you really appreciate the hug from above!

When I wrote my first book, *Hug Your Customers,* I wanted everyone in the organization to feel recognized, for it was their book as much as it was mine. So Pamela hatched a great idea that I readily endorsed. She took the list of all full-time associates who had been with us for longer than five years—nearly two hundred people—and searched the text of *HYC* to make sure that each name was mentioned at least once. If a name wasn't already in the book in one of our truc stories about our hugging culture, she replaced a generic name such as Mrs. Gotrocks with Mrs. Rapoport, to represent Trish Rapoport. Sometimes, she combined the first name of one of our associates with the last name of another associate, just to make sure that everyone got mentioned at least once in the book. I've even heard an associate say, "Check out page forty-two, that's my name. I'm in the book!"

Another big thing is to be flexible, especially when a person's living situation changes. Belinda, for instance, was a great seller for us at Richards. Then Peter, her husband, moved his business to Atlanta. We were reluctant to lose her, and she was reluctant to lose us. So we designed a compensation arrangement that allowed her to commute from Atlanta. She worked with us—longer daily hours than usual—from Wednesday through Saturday. When she needed to, she stayed in a nearby hotel, where we negotiated a very favorable rate, and spent the other three days in Atlanta. She did this for several years, until she and her husband felt that three days a week together just weren't enough, which we of course understood. But while she commuted, her sales were as great as ever and she was grateful that we could be so flexible. We had our first nine-hundred-mile commuter!

Then the nicest thing happened recently—for us and for them—when Peter's business brought them back to New York. Of course, we took Belinda back in a heartbeat and we're all hugging each other anew—with a much shorter commute for Belinda!

THEY'RE ALL SUPERSTARS

I sometimes get asked, How do you recognize "mediocre" associates? In other words, how do you make someone who isn't a top superstar feel great and never want to leave?

My first response, and it's a strong one, is that we simply don't hire mediocre people. Our mind-set is that everyone we hire is great in his or her own way. Or they have the potential to go forward with great coaching and practice. These associates are the backbone—in many cases the heart and soul—of the business. Every day, every week, they come in, they do their best, and they go the extra mile.

Naturally, there are some exceptional superstars—certain people sell a lot more merchandise than others or sew the intricate alterations like handmade buttonholes or press garments perfectly and with lightning speed. So what you do to make everyone else feel good inside is recognize that every individual is working at the height of their capabilities, and that they are always trying to become better by listening, learning, and growing. And when they accomplish something significant—when they hit a home run or they have five singles in a game, as they surely do—you make a huge deal out of it. When we see or hear that one of our "backbone of the organization" people hugs a hugger or hugs a customer, we jump up and down and they actually feel like a superstar, because indeed they are.

Bruce Kelly tells me that it's sort of like "batting ninth or even twelfth for the Yankees; it's such a great team to be on, because no matter where you are in the batting order you feel like a winner!"

So take a picture of both your superstars and your backbone players, and each one of them will feel they are an extra-special part of the team.

CHAPTER 30

Rewards Should Be Enduring

What could be more annoying than to have the greatest performance month of your life the very moment that your company discontinues its Associate of the Month Program? Instead of a nice little bonus and a flattering picture of you hanging on the wall, you get nothing. Just bottled-up resentment.

One thing we've learned, and it's been a little painful at times, is that certain rewards programs to recognize associates don't work very well, especially if they're temporary. It's difficult to eliminate a program that you've introduced as a reward without experiencing backlash. Once something has become an accepted part of the routine, discarding it makes people feel unhugged, and that's the last thing you want. People tend to possess very long memories about perks they no longer have.

I call these takeaways.

For example, we used to give clothing allowances—one or

two suits per season or per year for each sales associate. But as our business grew it got extremely complicated to manage. How expensive should the suits be? How do you equalize the allotment between men and women? And how do you thank the nonsellers who don't often wear suits? It got to be such a hassle and the accounting was such a nightmare that we finally said "no más." My memory is that we may have compensated those associates by increasing their bonuses or salaries to cover the takeaway, but to this day those that had clothing allowances remember that we took away those suits and dresses, and it probably still irks some of them.

The same thing happened with getting birthdays off. For quite a while, we gave associates the day off on their birthdays. Other companies do it, too—I know Xerox does—but eventually it didn't seem to make a lot of sense to us and it got a little disruptive, especially when someone's birthday fell on the Saturday before Christmas! We scrapped the idea when we revisited our entire policy of personal days and time off. But again, it bothered some people and left a lingering bad taste.

I wasn't entirely kidding about the Associate of the Month Program. We actually had one for a quite a while—and I still like the idea—but we let it lapse. Over time, we realized that it's very cumbersome to execute. Who was really going to be in charge of picking the person? What were the criteria? What symbol of appreciation do you give? (We used to put names on a plaque and award a $100 certificate.) It was a popular program, but the person in charge dropped the ball for a couple of months, and then it was over. And for some, it was sorely missed.

So you have to be very careful. When you institute a repeating hug, consistency, matching the recipient with the criteria, and doing your level best to make sure that you're giving the recognition to the right person at the right time require a huge commitment. Make sure you're going to be able to sustain it. If you start something and then stop it, it looks like you didn't find it meaningful. The negative effect of eliminating a hug is always more powerful than the positive effect of adding it. It's just human nature.

Certain takeaways, of course, are far more consequential than a monthly plaque. Think about the companies that have canceled or in some way cut their pension plans, like some of the major airlines. When a company is in financial peril, these things happen, but people still don't always understand.

For the last few years, in addition to the 2-4-6-8 bonus program, we've been able to give a discretionary bonus when our fiscal year ends. And we've done it because, as Bill Mitchell says, "It's the right thing to do." We've had some excellent years and we wanted to share the financial bounty with all of our associates. And, of course, this hug has been extremely well received!

The first year, it was a surprise hug. I dare say last year also. But I just know that if we have an okay year, or even a down year, and we don't award the bonus, some people may feel it's a takeaway.

It helps tremendously that we're a transparent company, and so our associates know as readily as management does if sales taper off, and thus I trust most people would understand. But with niceties not tied to financial performance, you have to deliver them consistently—and for a long time (I was going to say forever, but nothing is forever)!

So you need to find several things that you will do for at least five or more years on a regular basis and stick to them! One of my dreams is to some day allow paid sabbaticals for a month or two as a standing reward for long-time associates, something that has become popular at various other companies. But we can't start a program like that unless we can be certain that it makes sense and that we can keep it going. And I haven't really invited others to become involved in this idea—not yet—and maybe there will be lots of reasons sabbaticals wouldn't work well for us.

And more than ever, we're determined that our recognition hugs remain enduring.

CHAPTER 31

Fair Is Not Always Equal

Everyone has heard the expression "Different strokes for different folks." To us, it's another way of saying, "Fair is not always equal," and it's something that we heartily believe in. It's a huge and important topic, and it's one that everyone at Mitchells/Richards/Marshs discusses and some even debate.

We learned this phrase and concept from David Bork, our family business expert, who outlined it for us at one of our family business meetings. Years ago, he told us the obvious: everyone in the family is not created equal in terms of abilities. One's more analytical. One's more personable. One's a better putter or has a better drop shot. We have different skill sets and over time we've learned that we each have contributed in our own unique fashion to the success of the business, and we have been rewarded and recognized accordingly. Not all equally, but hopefully fairly.

And we have tried to apply this same notion to our associates. People earn different salaries, bonuses, responsibilities, and positions. And, from time to time, various people want something extra, a hug of some sort. And because they're different folks, their desires differ. For example, Sandra asked for the day before Christmas off, because for her it's a very special evening when she cooks dinner for her entire family. After this was fully explained to the powers that be, we said, "Of course." We know there are many other people in the stores who cook dinner on Christmas Eve, but somehow they manage—they may instead like time off to go to a basketball game or the opera, or their mum is visiting from England, or their great-aunt Edna is in town. In short, different strokes for different folks.

It's also true that some people are scheduled to come in later, while others are scheduled to leave earlier. At meetings, some people are singled out for important contributions. In all these instances, though, the associates who received the flexible schedules or who were celebrated earned it.

Like with everything else, you have to be entirely transparent on this issue. You can suffer some highly negative impact if you don't make it clear why someone is getting a special reward. Otherwise, it will seem that you are promoting a culture of inequality rather than what we like to think of as a culture of fairness.

The critical point that we underscore is that no one is *entitled*. We learned this concept, too, from David Bork. And the *no one is entitled* principle includes family.

This is a big thing. Frank, Rita, John, and Jeff have all gone to Italy with the buyers. They weren't entitled to go, they earned the trip through their outstanding performance. It's not that much different from the notion that everyone has the same fair chance at getting the parking place closest to the door—they just have to be there first or have broken a leg skiing.

The bottom line is that everyone has an opportunity to receive special hugs that will motivate them and help them to achieve their goals in their own way. Equal opportunity, not unlike the ideals of American democracy, means everyone has the same access to the tools to drive the business. It also means they all have access to senior management, so anyone in the organization can approach us and therefore be exposed to potential future opportunities.

The challenge is that until everyone understands the way this works—really "gets it"—it may appear that it is unfair to allow someone to have a flexible schedule. Thus you have to stress to everyone that those hugs were earned, and that they can earn them, too. Then when people say, "Why is this person getting this and I'm not?" the other associates say, "Think of what Todd or Scott has done special for you."

Obviously, it takes maturity and time to understand and accept the reality that when your day or month comes you'll get that extra hug just like your teammate. Maybe even two or three hugs that day or year. People receive their special hugs at different moments. It's sort of what happens as children grow up. An older sibling gets a bigger allowance and gets to stay up until nine, while his brother has to be asleep at eight. The younger brother wails, "That's not fair." But it is, because when he reaches his brother's age in another two years, he'll get that bigger allowance and nine o'clock bedtime, too. They're not equal at the moment, but they are being treated fairly.

What's crucial is the balance you strike. You want to try to distribute a hug here and a hug there so that everyone on the team feels that they are special and that they are indeed receiving different strokes because they are different folks. When individuals understand this balance, they perform as a team and the team excels and sells.

That's part of the magic we have.

It is true that you need to furnish a little context now and then to help people understand how fair is not always equal. A few years ago, one of the sales associates said to me, "This tailor makes more than I do!" And I said, "You know, I'm not going to tell you whether he makes more than you do or not, but if you want to go down to the tailor shop, please go ahead! We need great tailors."

And, of course, that produced a speedy end to the conversation.

Many years ago, one of our associates had done an outstanding job, and during his annual review I gave him what I thought was a very sizable raise and bonus. And while he was grateful for the increased compensation, he really felt that he deserved a lot more and told me so. And he stressed that he felt like a partner in our business, part of the extended family.

Now, it so happened that I had just personally signed a note for a loan for the new store that we were building for what was a lot of money in those days. And I remember exactly where I was sitting when I said, "Bob, I'll tell you what, I'm so delighted you feel like you are a partner, and in many ways I share that feeling. So you know what, I'll give you that additional bonus you'd like, but I want you also to cosign the note for the new store, and be sure to let your wife know. Now, you know and I know we are going to pay that money back and the store is going to do well, or I wouldn't have been willing to sign personally myself. But remember there is always a chance that we won't do so well, or Bill and I could get run over by a beer truck and then the bank could take my house and yours and all the money we've saved for our sons' educations!"

So anyway, he went home that night and discussed the situation with his wife. He came back the next day and said he was extremely grateful for the very fair raise and bonus I'd originally suggested!

We're well aware that the nonsellers—our buyers, our shipping and receiving people, our marketing people, and so forth—occasionally feel that the sellers get all of the attention, accolades, and special rewards, which of course in the big picture means the nonsellers do not feel hugged and that things are not fair. So at times, as the king of Siam said, "T'is a puzzlement" how to execute special treats.

The answer is to make sure you dole out appropriate rewards to nonsellers—as long as they earn them. If you can hear them say, "Wow, I went to a charity event because I love them," and another associate say, "I went to a Yankee game because I love sports" or "I went to a Ralph Lauren fashion show" or "I watched my son play hockey" or "I drove my daughter to college on a busy Saturday," then you've successfully achieved your different strokes for different folks. Focus and learn who likes what and deliver. Consistently.

Ultimately, if you personalize the relationships, you make everyone feel very satisfied in what they are doing, and in their contribution to the team. If they feel hugged by their immediate peers and acknowledged by managers, then it's a nonissue. They recognize that Ginger is a grandmother and Alana has a two-year-old being potty trained, and they might pass by the store when we are closed on a Sunday and see Rita with a client or Gail staying late in the evening to accommodate her best customer.

It's important, of course, to also have Marlene and Gary and other sellers thank Lauren and Kristen for getting the merchandise expedited and thank Ed in shipping and receiving for ticketing the merchandise.

There's no question that explaining and executing the fair is not always equal concept is a huge challenge in our culture—and in any culture. It's a challenge but it's worth it.

And I believe it's absolutely essential to preserve team harmony and productivity in a hugging culture.

CHAPTER 32

Hugging Around the Clock

Associates are people, and when they head home they lead enriching lives but also sometimes encounter personal trials, and we can't forget that. If you develop a personalized relationship with your associates, that relationship doesn't end at the office door. It reaches all the way into their houses and it functions twenty-four hours a day. And so you have to support them when things get bumpy. It's part of how you recognize them. Furthermore, it's part of personalizing the professional relationship.

That's why our managers and human resources people urge our associates, "Don't leave your problems at home. Let's talk about them and let us help you with them."

Of course, there are boundaries, and at all times you need to be extraordinarily sensitive and respectful of this and their private lives. But when associates reach out, you need to be there.

Like many companies, we have an Associate Assistance Program (notice we don't call it Employee Assistance), and we have had it for many, many years. Along with our human resources department, these professionals will gladly listen to problems or personal challenges in total confidentiality. In unusual cases, when we sense a nagging issue, we'll recommend that a person seek assistance, or, as is more often the case, they go to our AAP without our knowledge.

We're told that many smaller or medium-size companies don't usually extend this benefit to their associates. In our community, we were one of the pioneers. We have representatives come in at least once a year, much like we do for our insurance benefits, and share that there is a service that is provided free to our associates for a prescribed number of visits. From the service providers, associates can get advice and counseling on substance abuse, spousal abuse, elderly care, financial assistance, children, pressures at work, or other stresses. It's all anonymous and done in complete confidence, unless the associate wants us to know. Often we find out when the situation has been resolved and they thank us for caring. We do meet with the AAP coordinators regularly to make sure that they are truly hugging our huggers consistent with our culture.

But when problems arise, everyone who works with us is ready with an available shoulder to lean on. Sue Mitchell, Bill's wife, has nicknamed Bill "Florence Nightingale," since Bill has touched many associates over the years by helping them find the right doctor at the right time. I can't estimate the number of occasions when people haven't been able to see a doctor because he wasn't accepting new patients. Bill or one of the Mitchells gets on the phone, and, voilà, they have an appointment the next week.

In the old days, before the advent of associate assistance programs and the store was much smaller, we'd loan our people extra money so they could buy a house or put their kids through college. Today, of course, we still care and want to help associates, so we use other avenues, such as our community contacts, where we can facilitate loans for associates with friendly financial institutions. And it's been a long-standing practice for us to help associates find jobs for their kids and help them get elderly parents into nursing homes. Some people want this to be public support and some want it to be private, and respecting the difference is hugging your huggers.

JM Family Enterprises, a Florida-based Toyota distributor and Lexus dealer, has formalized this sort of aid and gotten the whole company involved. It maintains an Associates Helping Associates fund. It contributed $25,000 to get it going and matches associate contributions dollar for dollar. The fund then gets tapped when an associate has an emergency and nowhere to turn.

When an appliance and electronics chain became concerned about the impact marital stresses were having on its associates, it began offering marriage training classes. To keep things upbeat, it even orchestrated a fun takeoff of *The Newlywed Game* derived from the famous TV show to help spouses better understand and appreciate each other.

At our business, Bill is almost a one-man associate help center, for kindness is truly embedded in his genes. Years ago, Paul, one of Domenic's two sons, was riding his motorcycle and it skidded on rain-slick roads and went under a UPS truck. Paul was in dreadful shape. First, it looked as if he wouldn't live, then that he would lose a leg. The moment he heard, Bill was making calls, getting the finest doctors in the area working on the case, and then he rushed to the hospital to console Domenic. The doctors performed miracles, and Paul remained intact. He's now a police officer in Florida.

One day, Phyllis said in a clear but trembling voice, "He's gone. He just vanished from his home. He always called before and came back, but it's four days and Stanley and I are scared to death. Bill and Jack, please help us."

She was talking about her special-needs son. Of course, we both went into high gear, using our contacts in our community. Bill—Mr. Westport—called Mike Barrett, the retired chief detective of the Westport Police Department. I contacted my next-door neighbor, Ed Adams, who just happens to be an FBI agent. Quickly and quietly, our two friends went the extra hugging mile and located Phyllis's son, safe and sound.

Phyllis regularly tells her customers and friends, "In one hour, the Mitchells did something we weren't able to do in four days. It was amazing."

Another time, Pam Miles was in my office, which boasts a wall of windows facing the hallway, and she looked up and spotted a manager on the phone, obviously distraught, because she was crying. When the woman hung up, Pam went over and offered her a Kleenex and invited her to sit down in my office and avail herself of some privacy.

She ended up telling Pam that what she really needed was a hotel room for the night to cool down. She explained that she had to work tomorrow but really didn't want to go home that night. Without asking anything more, Pam said, "Sure. I'll put it on the company card. Let me just tell someone that I'm doing this. Todd is here today so I'll let him know."

Pam also suggested that the woman talk to the human resources person who was working that day at Mitchells. She then made the hotel reservation, informed Todd without going into detail, and that was that. Although she saw the woman the next day at work, Pam never discussed the episode with her again. By helping her out in a moment of great need and respecting her privacy, Pam gave her a huge hug. We'd do the same thing for anyone who works with us.

THE HUGS COME BACK

Associates don't forget this concern. Years ago, a man named Ted came to work with us at Mitchells. He was in his mid-sixties, a gem of a guy who did pressing. During his time with us, he had quite a roller-coaster experience. One day, I heard a big celebration going on in the shop. "Ted won the lottery!" was the cheer. Alas, it turned out to be a false alarm. He had read the numbers wrong. As you can imagine, he was both embarrassed and deeply disappointed.

A year or two later, he suffered a life-threatening stroke and was in the hospital for months. He was left with a crippled leg, but he regained his positive attitude and periodically came in to schmooze with his friends in the store.

One day he hobbled in with a huge smile, looking for Dad. He was in Florida, but I got him on the phone. They chatted for a few minutes, punctuated with lots of laughter. When they finished, I was curious and asked Ted, "What was that all about?"

"Oh, Jack, this time I really did win the lottery," he said. "Over a million! I didn't tell a soul until I had the cash in the bank. You see, Jack, when I was down and out and in the hospital, your mom and dad came in to visit and cheer me up, as did so many of my friends at Mitchells. It meant everything to me, since I had only one niece alive in my blood family. And your dad leaned over and in his gentle voice said, 'Ted, are you okay? I mean, I can see you will live and go home, thank God, but do you need financial help—a loan to pay your bills or whatever?' I was all choked up, and said, 'I'm fine, I've saved all my life for a challenging period like this, but thank you and Norma very much, from the bottom of my heart. You're simply wonderful.' So your dad was the first person in the store to hear my good news, and I said to him, 'Ed, I'm a rich man now, do you need a loan?'"

We both chuckled. And Ted went on to share his good fortune and celebrate with his extended family in the tailor shop, because they had been so caring.

While I love Ted's story, what made me feel equally proud is when a key associate shared with me in front of a number of other associates, "You know what's really neat about this hugging culture? It's that I know that whatever the nature of my personal or family challenge the Mitchells and our managers are there for us."

That's because we're hugging around the clock!

CHAPTER 33

When the Passion Goes

Every time we hire someone, we hope it's for that person's career, and that could be five or fifty-five years. Most of the time, that's exactly what happens. But not always. People change—or don't change. And we make mistakes. Or they do.

For me, firing someone is not only difficult but it's the worst thing I have to do. It's so sad to see someone you've trusted steal from you or not perform as you had hoped. Whenever I have to tell someone to leave, I don't sleep, sometimes for nights.

But a person with truly unacceptable behavior has to either change or go, no matter how much a superstar he or she might be, because if someone is pulling down the rest of the team or otherwise creating chaos within the team, it isn't fair.

We never terminate people hastily—unless we're forced to. Sad to say, despite all we do to try to enhance our hugging culture, people do steal. Of course, when we find out someone is stealing from us, we act swiftly and their actions are reported to the police and they are immediately gone. Period.

Other than with criminals, though, we strongly believe in giving people second and third and even fourth chances—if they're willing to stay and change. That's what support is about. For example, if someone needs help being nice and positive, we would privately help him notice when he was being negative, and right after hearing him handle a situation we would use the feedback process and ask, "May I give you some feedback?" Through continued team leader reinforcement, the person would glean information and experience on how to become positive. Over time, there would be less and less need for feedback as the person got more and more encouragement on his positive mind-set.

Alas, for many reasons, not all third and fourth chances work out, and then you have to set a limit and take action. If an associate doesn't fit in, no matter what interventions you try, the sooner it ends the better, for both the business and the person. In several cases, I have found that it was really the best thing for the associate. The person found a new culture where he could feel comfortable.

When it comes to separating with people, we have devised some straightforward principles that we abide by. In our view, people must go for four reasons:

1. Stealing: In the old days, we were nice guys and we just fired them. But Bill and I learned, and our sons and other leaders concur, that these people have to be arrested and *prose-cuted,* and that's what we've been doing for years now. Other-wise honest associates suffer.

And stealing means not only swiping merchandise but cheating on discounts or giving discounts to others. And, again, you have to be consistent here. The same standards ap-ply to everyone. Our associates trust us that no matter how im-portant someone might be in other areas of the business, if they are doing something illegal they will answer to the police.

2. Someone violates the trust to get along with fellow associ-ates, customers, or vendors: If a person continues to be con-frontational and nasty, she has to go. For example, if a sales associate is "stealing" customers from other associates after re-peated warnings, then she can't continue with us. We have lost a few—but very few—associates over this issue.

One man had all of the credentials to be a great leader and seller. He said the right words, but in the end he was a by-the-rules, black-and-white, authoritarian manager. And he got so frustrated that we wouldn't support him in disciplining and punishing some of the sellers that he just quit. We were relieved that he did, because he clearly wasn't a fit in our culture. I'm sure this bright young man has found a suitable position some-where else—perhaps in the Marine Corps.

More than thirty years ago, when he first assumed the lead-ership of the tailor shop, Domenic fired three or four tailors with diplomas from European trade schools. Not only were they not nice but they were often dishonest because they didn't do all of the alterations that Dom asked them to do. Customers would end up with dresses that weren't lengthened and suits that were still too wide in the waist, and the other tailors had to make amends. Had to go!

3. Someone is incompetent in his or her skill sets: This outcome is particularly disappointing, because we believed in the person and thought he was up to the job. It means we misjudged someone, or the person was very accomplished at conning us into believing he was more qualified than he was. Because of our exhaustive hiring process, it's extremely rare that this happens. When it does, I always say to myself, "How did I not see this fatal flaw?"

4. An associate doesn't change: This happens in different forms. Sometimes an associate has been a wonderful performer, but gets worn out and loses the passion to listen, learn, and grow. It's a very sensitive area, and a formidable challenge. We really try hard to continue to motivate and enable all of our people to grow, but we really do review the brutal facts. If people are not growing, or not hugging, then they are asked to go elsewhere, because otherwise they will fall behind and drag others with them. Candidly, many of them leave on their own because it's so obvious that they no longer fit in our culture.

Another way this happens is when an individual who has put in years of service—couldn't be nicer, couldn't be more trustworthy, you've rewarded him in the past—just can't keep up with the new emerging pace of our business, even though he tries. The person is not capable of adapting to change. This is always the hardest case. Yet we can't keep people who let the world speed by them. Several of us grandparents have had to become "modern" and adapt to new technology—learn how to hug through e-mails, how to tell DVDs from CDs, how to personalize personal relationships as well as professional relationships by using the latest tools. But, alas, for reasons we can't always fathom, not everyone can do it.

For an organization to grow, its people must grow. You don't have to grow every week or every month—but every year, for sure. And you don't have to grow in every area, but you need to do so in some areas, or at least in one important area. This is why we've created the Mitchell Hug University, so we do all we can to coach our people to grow and so they can learn from one another.

BE POLITE

When someone is let go, it should certainly be done in a caring and humanizing fashion, especially in cases where the trust hasn't been exploited. It's astonishing how cruel companies get—like notifying people that they're being laid off by e-mail or registered letter or text message. Imagine sitting at dinner with the family, passing the beans, and your cell phone alerts you to a text message: "Sorry, you have been terminated. Clean out your desk by nine tomorrow."

There's only one way to deliver bad news, and that's in person, face-to-face.

You also hear about managers bringing in armed guards to escort people out. It's totally uncalled for, except in extreme circumstances. You have to realize that customers who hear about dismissed people being treated shabbily may not want to remain your customers. And promising people may not be inclined to come to work for you.

So we insist on the same courteous manners we so firmly abide by. One of our principles, though, is that if someone leaves to better himself (at least from his perspective), and even if he's not joining a competitor, we generally ask the person to go immediately. We say this politely, of course, but we prefer that he leaves the same day and takes all of his personal belongings and leaves us all of his professional belongings. We've learned the hard way that this works best. You don't quit our culture without a great deal of thought, and once the decision has been made that person will be dreaming about the new position, so his head is not with us.

No matter how nice we might be, how trustworthy we might be, how inclusive we might be, we know and acknowledge that we are not perfect. People do have a few gripes or critical comments, and these departing associates might blast them out, since they feel they have nothing to lose. It's much better to wish these people farewell nicely and bid them good luck and mean it, and then have them leave and not come back through the back door. They're always welcome through the front door.

If a person is switching to another industry, that's different. For example, we had a young man named Larry G., who did an outstanding job at Richards and decided to become a stockbroker. We threw a wonderful good-bye party for him, as we've done for others in similar circumstances and, of course, when people retire.

Sometimes we've had to let people go who were very nice, but they just couldn't grow as the store grew. In these cases, we do everything we can to have them leave with great dignity and respect. But—and this is important—I don't believe anyone should get pushed out the door because of age. I simply don't think in terms of people's ages. My vision isn't so poor that I can't recognize if someone is in his twenties or in his sixties. But my mindset is not that the sixty-year-old may have only ten more years with us or that the seventy-year-old maybe only one or two. It's all about how the individual can contribute to the store—period.

There's a difference between being positive and realistic. Jim MacLaren is a motivational speaker and author, noted for his record-breaking performances in the marathon and Ironman triathlon after having his left leg amputated below the knee. He helped me clarify the distinction when he told me, "I'm not a fool. I can't physically do everything, but my mindset is I can do anything!" I love that phrase. I like people who think they can do anything.

So we believe that you can be very productive as a twenty-five-year-old and as a seventy-five-year-old. Realistically, you get a dash more tired at seventy-five than at twenty-five, but the seventy-five-year-old has fifty more years of experience that might enable him to work a dash wiser.

So we think people should work as long as they have the passion and can contribute. Dad continued with us in a consulting capacity until he was almost ninety-nine, and we would have loved to have had his wisdom for a few more years, or even decades. He always believed he could do anything! Dad was a visionary and we very much model our "ageless culture" on his example.

CHAPTER 34

Welcome Back,
Welcome Home

A few years ago, Cathy Fotinopoulos, who was Linda's assistant for years, left with Linda's blessing and all of our good luck and best wishes to open up a small women's shop in Bethel, Connecticut, where she was living.

Often, when someone leaves a company, it's as if the person died or otherwise vanished from the face of the earth as far as the company is concerned. Even people who have been great associates, when they walk out the door for the last time they become ghosts. Well, not to us.

During the first holiday season Cathy's store was open, Linda and I were trying to figure out our Secret Santa presents for fellow associates when we got the idea to get in the car one Sunday and drive over to Bethel, about thirty minutes from Westport, and visit Cathy in her new store. So we did just that.

We had a wonderful time chatting and laughing with her, and naturally we also bought a few things.

Not that long afterward, maybe two years since her departure, Cathy called Linda and said she was closing her store and asked if we would take her back. In a snap, Linda said, "Of course." She took the words right out of my mouth.

One day soon after her return, I was curious and I asked Cathy what had been the biggest hug she had ever gotten from the Mitchells, and she responded right away that it was when Linda and I came to her store that Sunday. Her point was "You didn't have to do that. I wasn't even working for you."

She loved our hug for what it was—a simple, personal, genuine reminder that we cared about her and her "baby." We happened to really like her, so even though she was thirty minutes away, we took the extra time to go to her.

What's the moral? Keep recognizing great people after they leave, because it's a hug and because we've learned that one day you may want to welcome them back.

Take Beverly Martin, another wonderful example. After being the manager of the women's department at Mitchells for years, Bev retired. To most companies, retirees are yesterday's news. Well, we continued to stay in touch. And I continued to send her and her husband, Jerry, an orchid plant during the holiday season, along with a friendly note, as a symbol of our personal relationship and to thank her for all the years she gave to us.

For a while, Bev tried her skills in real estate by "flipping" houses. Then she came out of retirement and actually worked for a competitor of sorts, the women's department at Saks Fifth Avenue in Greenwich. They weren't a huge competitor of Mitchells, because of the distance they were from Westport, and we didn't yet sell women's clothing at Richards.

But then we decided to build a new store and add a women's department to Richards, and we began wooing her to join our new team. Although the orchids weren't the key reason, she mentioned that our hug of continuing to send her a little expression of our appreciation, which was always genuine, did help her decide to return. I was blown away, and it bolstered my view of flower power!

And, wow, what a substantial contribution she has made to building the women's business with Scott. In six short years, we've been told, we've become the dominant women's designer clothing and accessories team in Greenwich.

So in some cases a former associate calls us, and in other cases we call them. It happens different ways, but the common denominator is that we never stop hugging.

Of course, you don't welcome everyone back who wants to return. Others have left us to join competitors and done so in a way that broke the trust or the personal relationship. There are actually very few of these people who have asked to come back, but when they have, we've had to say no—in a nice way of course.

Who, then, should you take back? It's pretty simple.

1. They left for a personal reason that was clear to us and it was best for them personally, and in some cases professionally.
2. They joined a company that wasn't a direct competitor.
3. We valued their contribution during their career with us.
4. Most important, they embrace the hugging culture— hugging the huggers and hugging the customers, and all of the five guiding principles.

If they satisfy these criteria, then we say, "Welcome back, welcome home."

One of the most important reasons to welcome them back is that when people leave to do other things they usually acquire an even greater appreciation of our hugging style. They see another world, and usually it's not greener, and frequently it's pretty brown. Many years ago, Tony Gregorio, our head of shipping and receiving at Mitchells, left us. He thought he wanted to be "an executive in a suit." And that's what he became. A year or two later, it hit him that he had left the greatest job in the world. He realized, you are who you are. He asked to resume his old job and we welcomed him back. And the executive taste he sampled has allowed Tony to really help us grow from a small store to one of the largest specialty stores in the country—all by managing people in his sport shirt and jeans.

It happens like that often. When people return, full of gusto, they tend to make an even greater contribution and are even more positive about being with us once again. They've come home, and it makes them feel great.

So remember not to lock the door and pull down the shades when a terrific associate leaves. Keep that welcome mat at the door. You never know. You may want to hug him all over again.

HUGGING STUDY GUIDE #5

RECOGNIZE

It's not just money: People aren't motivated only, or even primarily, by money, but it's important to pay them wages and extra bonuses at least equivalent and preferably better than the competition, or else they'll feel you're chintzy.

Run their pictures: Use associates in your advertising, name planes after their kids, hold honorary dinners, do the special things that make people feel appreciated and special.

Rewards should be enduring: If you offer a reward program and then dismantle it, it leaves a bitter aftertaste that can persist for years to come, so don't start something you're not confident you can perpetuate.

Fair is not always equal: Associates aren't created entirely equal, so neither should their rewards be equal, but they should be fair. It has to be clear that you get what you earn—both in money and in extraordinary hugs of appreciation.

Support them when the going gets rough: Associates encounter difficulties outside of work—with relationships and addictions and missing children—and it's your responsibility to do all you reasonably can to help.

Not everyone works out: You hurt everyone when you keep poor-performing or disruptive associates, so they have to go: definitely and immediately if they steal, if they fail to get along with others, if they're incompetent, or if they don't change after they've been given ample opportunity.

Welcome them back: After people leave for other opportunities or retire, don't write them off as dead. They may want to come back home, and you may want them back.

I'm Going to Have Fun Today

When I get up each morning, even those days when my back's a little stiff and I was out a dash too late and another hour of sleep might have been soothing, I still feel great. Why? Because I look forward to going to work—after all these years, it's still a lot of fun. I look forward to hugging all of our great associates and customers, and being hugged back by them. I often start singing in my car. And then, as I waltz through the store, I get kidded about how happy I sound singing. I've got my ten pennies jingling in my left pocket to make sure I fit in ten hugs, and I'm usually still hugging away when they're already resting in the right pocket.

It's a terrific feeling to love your work because of a sense of accomplishment and because you feel valued. It's a feeling I, and all of us at Mitchells/Richards/Marshs, wish for everyone.

Can you imagine a world where every morning you come into

the office and everyone smiles and says, "Good morning, Carlos!" And then they shake your hand, celebrating something great that happened the other day. Your best friend at work wants to know if your son got a hit in the Little League game over the weekend, and you proudly report that he was three for three! It turns out you need to leave by noon because your daughter is starring in a ballet recital, and everyone says, "Enjoy the show!"

Can you imagine a place where your leader and your peers urge you to invest time with family and friends? Like when Amy went with Max for a long "college hunt" weekend, or when Sophia and her husband, Cappuccino Bob, spent quality time with their daughter when she needed them. Where, hey, they give you the day off for a special event like a twenty-fifth wedding anniversary, and they even treat you to dinner and flowers are waiting when you return home.

Can you imagine a place where a veteran player like Oscar, who cleans the floors, feels comfortable enough to share with the new associate—in Spanish—how even as a recovering alcoholic he feels intoxicated by the positive, personalized, passionate culture at our store?

Can you imagine a place where Arlyne, Rita, John, and Linda are chattering in the lunchroom about their passions—snorkeling and ballroom dancing and growing beets—while John shares how much he enjoyed being with Rita's son Nicholas, his new best friend (who happens to be only eight years old), who he met during his recent trip to Italy? And Judy mentions how thrilled she is to help cover the Hermès shop while Janet is visiting her granddaughter in Atlanta, and she can't wait to hear how big she has grown since her last visit. And Eric in receiving is telling Laura that, sure, he'll be over on Saturday to help her fix the brakes on her car, while John, our security man, tells Jay he'll be glad to tune his grand piano. And Bruce and Scott are mapping out plans to go, yes, bowling! There's so much laughing good cheer that you'd think they were at a party, and yet they're at work.

This is what a bona fide hugging-your-people environment feels like—every day, every week, every year. It's teammates supporting one another, respecting one another, having fun together.

This is not fantasy. This is how it is at Mitchells/Richards/Marshs. Through this hugging-your-people attitude and culture, we have grown from a $50,000 business to what industry leaders tell us is the largest independent upper-end specialty clothing store in the United States. And we're proud of that.

Can this be your company?

Of course it can.

It's not nearly as difficult as you may think.

The business world is a competitive, sonic-paced world. If you sit still, you're inhaling someone else's exhaust fumes. All leaders are extraordinarily busy. Accomplishing the things that I've spelled out in this book may at first blush seem overwhelming, one more program or priority to add to a list that keeps getting longer.

That's not the way to look at it. No company is at the starting line when it comes to hugging its people. Everyone is somewhere along the rewarding road to the ultimate destination, and many companies are well along, some of them just an exit or two away.

I'm sure that you'll realize that you're already doing some of the things we recommend. All you need to do is build on that foundation. Most of these techniques, as I've stressed, don't cost a cent. They're a matter of attitude. They don't require task forces or elaborate capital projects.

They require desire and passion.

You have to *want* to hug your people.

What you need to do is start with baby steps and keep on walking. Change will occur faster than you might imagine. Once you get the hang of it, it will be easier and far more fulfilling than you ever thought possible. And pass it along to others in your organization. It's not work—it's fun.

So get going. Be Nice and say thanks to someone in the office. Trust your colleagues. Instill them with Pride. Include your teammates. And Recognize them in a multitude of ways.

Five simple principles that can transform your experience, your company's soul, and its people's lives. Try them out—today, tomorrow, and forever—you will be happy and you won't be sorry. Flip your business priorities and go play the fabulous game of hugging, and certainly you won't want to stop.

Hugging our people has worked for us—it will work for you!

Once again, thanks for listening.

And lots of hugs!

Hugging Achievement Test
(HAT)

I used this fun technique in my first book, *Hug Your Customers*, and received lots of positive feedback and thought it would be worthwhile to reprise it here. You will, I trust, find it a good way to see where you are in building a hug-your-people culture. I've constructed a small test. Most of us don't like tests, but I assure you that this one can be really fun! Feel free to complete it at your leisure—it's strictly for your own benefit. From your answers, you should be able to get a good feel for where you're already doing a good job of hugging your people and be able to isolate areas where you need to try harder. It makes sense to take it again periodically, to chart your progress. Don't worry, there are no grades. I haven't given out an F yet. And since it's a take-home test, you're on the honor system. So give it a go! And enjoy!

1. Make a list of a dozen ways—small and large—that you are nice to associates at work and make them feel appreciated. Can you list twenty-five?

_____

_____

_____

_____

_____

2. What things do you do to make new hires feel welcome and comfortable? Do you have a probation period, or something warmer and more positive?

_____

_____

_____

_____

_____

3. How many associates do you know by name? (No peeking at your facebook.) List them. What things do you know about them? If you can list 150, you're an authentic hugger. If you can list 250, I can't wait to meet you.

_____

_____

_____

_____

_____

4. Do you have any close friends at work? If so, how many? How do you share and celebrate hugs together, during good times (weddings, birthdays, anniversaries, bar mitzvahs) and sad times (illnesses, funerals)?

_____

_____

_____

_____

_____

5. At work, do you have rules or expectations? What are your expectations and standards for the people you work with?

_____

_____

_____

_____

_____

6. Do you encourage people to have fun at work? How? Do you engage in organized games or events? What are five recent ones?

_____

_____

_____

_____

_____

7. Do you make a point to reconnect with associates, with others? When? At the beginning of meetings? In person? By e-mail?

Do you start and finish encounters and letters with something personal?

_____

_____

_____

_____

_____

8. Do you promote honesty at work? How do you do it? How else do you show your people that you trust them? Do you operate a New World or Third World culture? Do you share sales results, have transparent offices, have electronic calendars for everyone to see?

_____

_____

_____

_____

_____

9. Do you check up on people or check in with them? What are your principles regarding intrusive technology? Do you monitor associate e-mails and phone conversations?

_____

_____

_____

_____

_____

_____

10. How do you resolve conflicts among associates? Do you ignore them and pray they go away, or do you have a method to settle them?

_____

_____

_____

_____

_____

11. List five things that you do to build pride in your organization. Do you have a corporate mission statement? Is it displayed prominently? Do you have up-to-date technology? Do you have an organized educational program?

_____

_____

_____

_____

_____

12. Do you involve yourself in the community so your associates feel proud of your generosity? List ten causes and organizations that you contribute to.

_____

_____

_____

_____

_____

_____

13. Do you regularly invite others to help devise strategy and make decisions? How do you decide whom to invite? How do you invite them?

_____

_____

_____

_____

_____

14. When you solicit input from associates, how do you do it? How do you show that you really value it?

_____

_____

_____

_____

_____

15. Do you genuinely include associates in the decision-making process? How? And how do you communicate with others to involve them? Do you tell them what you think they need to know or what they want to know?

_____

_____

_____

_____

_____

16. Do you pay people as well as the competition? Do you give bonus hugs? Do you have competitions that allow outstanding people to earn extra money or rewards? Besides money, what are five ways that you recognize associates?

_____

_____

_____

_____

_____

17. Do you make it clear to everyone that while everyone isn't rewarded equally, they are treated fairly? How do you get that message across?

_____

_____

_____

_____

_____

18. Do you encourage associates to come to you when they are having challenges inside and outside work? How do you help them?

_____

_____

_____

_____

_____

19. Under what conditions do you let someone go? When would you welcome a former associate back?

_____

_____

_____

_____

_____

20. Based on your previous answers, what do you think are your hugging strengths and your weaknesses in building a hugging culture? First list the five hugging practices you excel at and how you plan to improve them. Then, list five that you don't do that you intend to put into practice today, this year.

_____

_____

_____

_____

_____

Good luck, warm hugs.

ACKNOWLEDGMENTS

People.

It's all about people, and so many people have helped assist and guide me through the process of writing this book. It's been an amazing journey! In Lake Louise, Boston, or Las Vegas, time and time again after I finished a *Hug Your Customers* speaking engagement, people have come up to me and thanked me for taking the time and energy and using my enthusiastic voice to write the book. It truly touches me deeply emotionally and intellectually, and makes me feel wonderful inside and out. They have encouraged me to continue writing about hugs in business and in life. Thank you so very much.

Linda Mitchell, my wife, continues to be the center of my universe. My deepest, warmest gratitude goes to her. She has done so very, very much for me and our family, and has given up so much of herself for others, each and every day. She has delivered so many hugs to so many associates over the years. She has mentored and tutored and shared and helped, giving 1,001 percent. In every sense, Linda epitomizes the five principles that are the foundation of this book. She has been a leader and a manager, and many times when a project or "buy" needs to be done, she executes it herself, which helps set the high standards for others. She has made more than her mark; we wouldn't have our women's business if it hadn't been for Linda. And more than anyone else in my life, she has challenged me on every detail and made me reach and grow both personally and professionally. Thank you, darling.

Linda has been my partner for life and for our family. Bill, my brother, has been my partner in business for over thirty-nine years, and I'm sure he still will be when we exit. His wisdom and matchless hugging abilities shine every day in our stores and on every page of this book. Bill is a hall-of-fame, world-class hugger of our people. Always has been, always will be. It's in his DNA. Often I've watched with great admiration how he makes every associate feel great. He's amazing.

Undoubtedly, we've learned to hug our associates from our parents, Ed and Norma Mitchell, when they founded the business fifty years ago. They set the standards upon which our hugging culture rests. Even though we've lost them, Mom and Dad's spirit remains with so many who work with us, and will continue to guide future generations.

I owe particular gratitude to our four sons, Russell, Bob, Todd, and Andrew. I love and like them all as individuals. They are all very bright, well-educated, fun young men to be with and of course to work with in our stores every day. I am thankful to them for their insightful advice, suggestions, and encouragement in the writing of this book. They've all made their positive, productive mark in nurturing their colleagues to grow into super huggers.

Come to think of it, *Hug Your People* and *Hug Your Customers* are like our sons, unique and special individually, yet connected. It's their working together with other family members and associates that helps create the magic of our hugging business culture.

To my wonderful daughters-in-law, Kathy and Karen, and partner, Isaac, tons of hugs for their support of our family businesses and my books.

I am also grateful to Bill and Sue's three sons, Scott, Chris, and Tyler, who all occupy leadership positions in our stores. Both Scott and Chris have done a fabulous job in their responsibility for new businesses, the hiring and the inspiring of the women at our Richards store, and the entire team at Marshs, respectfully. In addition, I deeply appreciate their support of this project and Tyler's positive, passionate encouragement.

Each family member, blessed with different talents and strengths, always seems to find room for new and exciting ways to continue the hugging culture and to raise the bar for hugging our people. I acknowledge this attribute with great pride.

Also, I acknowledge openly that there would not have been a *Hug Your People* book without all of you.

Special thanks goes to Ray Rizzo, who gave me the extra nudge to go for this new book. Ray has been there for me at every stage of my career as an author.

Emil Frankel, my longtime best friend; Joe Cox, our senior executive and team leader at Richards; and David Bork, our family business consultant, all read the manuscript and gave me valued input and advice. Thanks, guys.

Many thanks and big hugs to Alexandra Ramstrum, associate publicist, and Zareen Jaffery, my editor. She has been supportive from the day we began. And to Will Schwalbe, vice president and editor in chief, and an author himself, who believed in our hugging philosophy from the start, plus all my friends at Hyperion, thank you for your support.

A wonderful new friend and huge hugger, Grant Gregory, led us to Geoff Brewer, editorial director of *Gallup Management Journal*, whose enthusiastic response to reading the manuscript resulted in a referral to a fantastic addition to our team, Barbara Cave Henricks, who has become a trusted publicist and, along with her associates, has opened up new doors to promote the book.

I also want to extend my appreciation to Margret McBride, my literary agent, plus Donna, Anne, and Faye, her terrific team, who have supported me in every step.

A tremendous hug goes to Pamela Miles, who is simply a super person and a superstar hugger in our Hugging Your People culture. Pam is a tireless, talented executive who has contributed at every stage—literally to every sentence of *Hug Your People*. She began as my executive assistant years ago, and now is the director of business development for my books, speeches, and consulting. I deeply appreciate all she has done and continues to do for me and our fellow huggers, both those in our business and those that we touch and engage throughout the country and the world. As I've shared with others so many times, without her, I'd still be dreaming about writing *Hug Your People*. Thank you so much, Pamela.

Finally, words cannot express my thanks to the great Sonny Kleinfield, my collaborator. He is quiet, humble, gentle, funny, passionate, and simply a great person, with the highest level of personal and professional integrity. He is super bright and, wow, can he write. I miss him when I'm not writing. I somehow feel I need a Sonny fix to get reconnected. He has captured my voice so remarkably that often I don't know where I've written or where Sonny has done what I call the "Kleinfield Magic" to my principles and stories. And the nicest thing for me is that we've developed a friendship that extends beyond our professional collaboration on my books.

And that brings me to the ultimate center of the universe for our business. Big hugs to all the wonderful associates at Mitchells/Richards/Marshs, each one of them individually listed up front in the dedication, for sharing their stories about hugging and living the culture of this book every day. When they hug their teammates, that force is connected to hugging their customers and clients. We will never forget, ever, not for a minute, that we have a successful business because of you, our associates, and of course our vendors and customers.

Thank you, thank you, thank you. Hug, hug, hug.